Am I Called?

Also by Dave Harvey:

Rescuing Ambition

When Sinners Say "I Do"

"This is the fullest, most realistic, down-to-earth, and genuinely spiritual exploration of God's call to pastoral ministry that I know. I recommend it most highly."

J. I. Packer, Board of Governors' Professor of Theology,
Regent College; author, *Knowing God*

"Every generation needs a fresh army of gospel men with a sense of destiny in their hearts. They aren't looking for a job. They are following a call. God is setting them apart to pastoral service. Are you one of those men? Dave Harvey's wise book will help you answer that question."

Ray Ortlund, lead pastor, Immanuel Church, Nashville, Tennessee

"Discerning God's call with clarity is an ongoing challenge, but a necessary journey. Dave Harvey has written one of the most helpful, practical books on Christian calling that I've read. *Am I Called?* guides a wide range of readers, not just pastors, through God's call to ministry in their lives. I know I will be sharing *Am I Called?* with many in the years to come."

Ed Stetzer, Billy Graham Distinguished Chair for Church,
Mission, and Evangelism, Wheaton College

"The issue of the call to pastoral ministry is a complicated one, involving matters of character, technical ability, and the guidance of the Holy Spirit. In this book, Dave Harvey offers a good overview of the things that anyone contemplating the ministry needs to consider. In an accessible, conversational style, Dave guides the reader through the biblical teaching on this matter—carefully balancing the external and the internal aspects of the call. He also provides apposite anecdotes from church history to illustrate his points. Full of wisdom and wit, *Am I Called?* is a delightful and challenging book for potential ministers, their wives, and, indeed, those already in the ministry to read. Highly commended."

Carl R. Trueman, pastor, Cornerstone Presbyterian Church,
Ambler, Pennsylvania; Paul Woolley Professor of Church History,
Westminster Theological Seminary, Philadelphia

"As a young man, I wrestled with the issue Dave Harvey wisely and skillfully addresses in this book. I'm glad a generation of young men can find in these pages the help that I was looking for thirty years ago."

Bob Lepine, cohost, FamilyLife Today

"The history of the church is marked and marred by the 'ministries' of unqualified men. The reason I am glad to recommend *Am I Called?* is that Dave Harvey sets the call to pastoral ministry in the biblical context: the calling from God and the calling from and to a local church. May God use this book to raise up a whole new generation of men who are called, equipped, and competent for the work he (and we) have called them to."

Tim Challies, blogger, challies.com; author, *Do More Better*

"My appreciation for this book is matched only by a sense of frustration that it wasn't around when I was considering my call to pastoral ministry. Dave Harvey manages to explain and insist upon the biblical requirements for pastors without being discouraging or legalistic. Most importantly, the good news about Jesus is the heartbeat of this clear and engaging book. If you are considering entering into pastoral ministry, *Am I Called?* will act as a faithful mirror and friend. If you are already a pastor, it will renew your passion for raising up the next generation of ministers."

Mike McKinley, pastor, Sterling Park Baptist Church, Sterling,
Virginia; author, *Am I Really a Christian?* and *Church Planting is
for Wimps*

"According to the Apostle Paul, faithful gospel ministry must include entrusting that ministry to others who will carry it on. *Am I Called?* will be of immense help to both those wondering whether they are called into gospel ministry, and to the pastors in position to help them figure that out. I know of no other book that does the important, practical work this book gets done and does so well. *Am I Called?* is marked by both wise, practical insight and a strong gospel vibrancy. I will be putting this book to regular use with young men at my church, and I'm glad to be able to highly recommend it."

Mike Bullmore, senior pastor, Crossway Community Church,
Bristol, Wisconsin

Am I Called?

THE SUMMONS TO PASTORAL MINISTRY

·············· DAVE HARVEY ··············

FOREWORD BY MATT CHANDLER

CROSSWAY®

WHEATON, ILLINOIS

Cover design: Faceout Studio

Cover image: David Sacks Studio

First printing 2012

Printed in the United States of America

Unless otherwise indicated, Scripture quotations are from the ESV® Bible (The Holy Bible, English Standard Version®), copyright © 2001 by Crossway, a publishing ministry of Good News Publishers. Used by permission. All rights reserved.

All emphases in Scripture quotations have been added by the author.

Trade paperback ISBN: 978-1-4335-2748-7
PDF ISBN: 978-1-4335-2749-4
Mobipocket ISBN: 978-1-4335-2750-0
ePub ISBN: 978-1-4335-2751-7

Library of Congress Cataloging-in-Publication Data
Harvey, David T. (David Thomas), 1960–
    Am I called? : the summons to pastoral ministry / Dave
Harvey ; foreword by Matt Chandler.
       p.   cm.
    Includes bibliographical references and index.
    ISBN 978-1-4335-2748-7 (tp)
    1. Clergy—Appointment, call, and election. 2. Vocation,
Ecclesiastical. 3. Pastoral theology. I. Title.
BV4011.4.H37   2012
253'.2—dc23   2011039685

Crossway is a publishing ministry of Good News Publishers.

VP		27	26	25	24	23	22		
20	19	18	17	16	15	14	13	12	11

To the pastoral team of
Covenant Fellowship Church,
We few, we happy few, we band of brothers.

Contents

· · · · · · · · · · · · · · · · ·

Foreword

. . . .

Immediately after my conversion, I developed an insatiable appetite for the Scriptures. My personality, even from my earliest memories, was one of constant curiosity. I wanted and even needed to know how things worked. I would take apart and try to put back together anything I could get my hands on.

When the Father sent the Spirit to open my eyes and ears to the beauty of Jesus, that curiosity was redeemed. I wanted and again even needed to know how our faith—my faith—worked, so I read and studied and memorized and asked a thousand questions to the poor ministers at the First Baptist Church that God so graciously saved me in. It didn't take long for me to start answering the questions of the lost people with whom I was sharing my life—and more importantly the gospel. And my Christian friends started coming to me with questions also. Not knowing the answer simply fueled my curiosity, and I would try to find the answer.

About six months after my conversion, I started being asked to do some teaching, mainly at children's church, vacation Bible schools, and the like. My opportunities culminated in what was our "youth-led service," where I was asked by our pastor to preach the Sunday night service. I was simultaneously nervous and excited. I preached my guts out that night, and although in my opinion the sermon was poorly done and exegetically erroneous, the Spirit of God moved powerfully that night. The altars were filled with people repenting and surrendering their lives to Christ. After the service, several people came up and encouraged me by saying they thought I was "called" into ministry.

I got my first job as a youth pastor at a small Baptist church about nine months later, and it was a nightmare. I was ill prepared, didn't know what I was doing, didn't know how church worked, and was in a system I didn't understand or (if I'm honest) agree with. My walk with the Lord was suffering greatly; I had secret sin in my life and felt very, very alone. After a year, I left thinking I wasn't called and instead should go into law and simply teach a Sunday school class.

I believe in God's providence in all things, including his timing, but I can't help but believe that if Dave Harvey had written this book twenty years ago, his wisdom and knowledge of the Scriptures and pastoral experience could have saved me from a bunch of pain and loss. If someone had pressed me regarding my godliness or asked me hard questions about my thought life and what I was doing in private, instead of looking at my personality and ability to communicate, I might not have bled so much in those days for being dishonest and walking in blatant rebellion before our great King.

Chapter after chapter, Dave does a phenomenal job of outlining what needs to be considered for all of us, regardless of life position or background, to answer the question: *Am I called?* The book's first section sums up what the call is and how that call comes to us. The second section is filled with questions, most of which you must continue to ask even after you enter pastoral ministry.

Are you godly? What a question to consider! Oh, how much deeper and wider ministries would be if godly men were leading them!

How's your home? So many young men forget that to not lead your home well disqualifies you from leading the church (1 Tim. 3:4). I've noticed among men I respect in ministry that they have a strong understanding of this truth. Read that chapter slowly.

Can you preach? What a simple and profound question. Can you open up the living Word and proclaim it in power? Dave does a great job pressing on a subject that gets muddy quickly. I've rarely come across a young man who doesn't believe he can bring it like Spurgeon. You don't have to be Spurgeon (and let's face it, you're not), but you have to be able to "feed the sheep."

Can you shepherd? The chapter on shepherding is a breath of fresh air in a climate where the false dichotomy of preaching or shepherding seems to be growing. We're called to do both.

Do you love the lost? I couldn't be happier that Dave included a chapter on evangelism and hospitality. It calls us not just to point others toward engaging the lost world but to actually engage it ourselves.

Who agrees? People should see these things in you. You should be known for your godliness and for your love for your family, the Scriptures, people, seeing people saved, and shepherding people who are hurting, broken, and wounded.

Dave finishes the book with a chapter titled "While You Wait." A week doesn't go by when someone doesn't tell me they feel called but don't know what to do now. I had a long, drawn-out answer, but now I can simply hand them this book that you're holding.

This book is long overdue. Regardless of where you are in life, if the Spirit is pulling on you and you think that pull is toward pastoral ministry of any kind, let the Spirit of God—moving through the wisdom, experience, and knowledge of Dave Harvey—bring clarity to that tug.

Christ is all,
Matt Chandler
Lead Pastor
The Village Church

PART ONE

Approaching the Call

· · · · · · · · · · · · · · · ·

1

The Summons
As I See It

. . . .

Have you ever been summoned? In my elementary school, every classroom had a speaker mounted over the door. It crackled to life each morning, shaking us out of our slumber with all the delicacy of a caffeinated drill sergeant. But it also served a secondary, more diabolical purpose. If the principal wanted you in his office, your name was announced over the loudspeaker. Now remember this was back in the day when public humiliation ranked alongside arithmetic for a well-rounded education.

Each time a voice boomed forth from the box on the wall, I wondered whether my time had come for the long walk to the principal's office. Now I know eight-year-old minds rarely touch down on planet Reality, but I think there were kids summoned to his office who never returned. I'm serious. I could just imagine secret corridors from the principal's office to dungeons and torture chambers. What else could explain why some kids were so courteous and compliant? I figured those few who were called out were probably locked away forever. Someday they would reappear somewhere, a shell of their former selves, their lives forever changed by the heart-stopping summons from a loudspeaker.

. . . .

*A summons is a call away from
one thing and into another.*

. . . .

But then I grew older and learned that a summons can be a good thing. Like when the coach grabs you by the jersey and shoves you into the game, saying, "Let's see what you've got." Or an inconvenient thing, like the official county envelope announcing jury duty. A summons can also alter your life. Any of you guys remember the selective service? That's what they call a military draft once it leaves the marketing department. Countless young men have pulled a quaking hand from the mailbox with a draft notice—a government summons obligating them to report for duty.

Regardless of the situation, a summons is a call away from one thing and into another. This book is about a particular kind of summons, and I believe it's one of the most glorious and strategic a Christian man can experience: the call to pastoral ministry.

Who's This Book For?

But hang on. Before going further, I need to be straight up about whom this book is written for. *It's written for men who may someday be pastors.* You may be hungering to plant a church—

this book is for you. Maybe you're in Bible school or seminary right now—yep, it's for you too. You might be in a good job but wondering if you're called to preach and lead, or perhaps you're in a job you hate, or you have no job at all. Pull up a chair; you're in the right place. College student wrestling with a calling? Teenage boy trying to interpret some stirrings? Glad you're here. You might be doing campus ministry, or missions, or some other vocational Christian work. You da man. You might even be a pastor wondering if you really should be doing what you're doing. This book is also for you.

But don't get me wrong. This isn't a book for everybody. It's not a general book on Christian leadership, though if you're a leader you might benefit from it. I don't expect this book will gain much traction in the Christian women's market, and neither does my publisher! You see, I believe the Bible clearly teaches that the call to pastoral ministry is only for Christian men. I know you may disagree, and I know we live in a culture where limiting opportunities for pastoral ministry to one gender relegates one to the category of quaint relic, right next to jukeboxes and black-and-white TV. I'm not going to enter the fray of the argument about whether to ordain women—that's someone else's book.

But I would love for some women to read this book, women who aspire to support godly pastors and use their gifts to build the church under biblical leadership. And my wife, Kimm, wants every woman who's a pastor's wife, or wants to be, to read this as well.

One thing you'll notice about this book is that it's full of stories—tales of real men who heard and wrestled through their summons in different ways. Some are famous folks you may know; others are regular Joes just like you and me. But I want you to know something. The stories aren't here just to keep you from nodding off while you read. They're portals through which we see a vast ocean of grace for a man called to ministry.

. . . .

*God isn't haphazard in whom he calls
or what he calls a man to do.*

. . . .

You see, God isn't haphazard in whom he calls or what he calls a man to do. He doesn't appoint bureaucrats over his church; he appoints men—flesh-and-blood, boneheaded mistake factories like you and me. He takes an ordinary guy, carves out his character, grants some grace, trains him with trials, zaps him with zeal, and corners him in his circumstances. Then you've got a pastor. That's a story worth telling—a story about grace.

How do I know? Well, let me tell you my story.

God's Project

Raised in a traditional denomination, I knew God was real. He just seemed sort of irrelevant. The church I attended did little to persuade me otherwise. An organ, plenty of gray-haired folks singing from hymnals, and a twenty-minute sermon typically left me wishing I had my twenty minutes back. In my pubescent mind, this ensemble had "snore" written all over it.

So I bailed. I did the jock thing through high school and

partied my way straight into college. I was a rock-n-roll-lovin', Steelers-rootin', homework-avoidin' dude. Rowdy friends and great weekends made for average grades. I don't have grand confessions of destruction and despair. In fact, my conversion story starts with a pretty unspectacular theme: I was having a great time living my life my way.

And it worked for me—for a while. But a life of self-indulgence is like a steady diet of Oreo cookies. Sure, it tastes great, but it never really satisfies the appetite. Crazy times and couch crashing eventually started to get stale. I began to starve for something more. Questions of meaning began knocking on the door of my party with annoying regularity. If there really is a God, what does that mean for me? What should I do with the life I've been given? What really surprised me—even haunted me—is that the questions were God questions, questions that didn't leave when I turned out the light—because it was God himself doing the asking.

In 1979, I was converted. Don't ask me when or where—I honestly don't know. I'm sure those answers will be supplied shortly after I shed this mortal shell. For now, I've got the year right. I think. Maybe it's more important to say I've sought to follow Christ faithfully for something like thirty-three years. Twenty-six of those years have been in full-time ministry. And that's the story I really want to tell here.

As a new believer, I was pretty full of myself. You're probably thinking, "Of course he was proud, he was under thirty!" Nah . . . it was, shall we say, slightly more pronounced. I figured God scored a pretty serious asset in converting me. In Dave's world, where reason and humility rarely came out of hibernation, I was God's first-round draft choice, a serious acquisition. I was gonna be a playmaker from day one. I mean, just imagine what a C-average, ex-jock could do to the kingdom of darkness. The mere possibilities made Satan shudder, or so I thought.

In other words, I had issues. I was arrogant, self-indulgent, selfishly ambitious, impatient, and instinctively rebellious against authority—and again, this was post-conversion!

And you know that internal device that prevents people from saying the sinful or stupid things they're thinking? Mine was busted for years. Once the pastor of our church wisely inquired why I only attended the church but never joined. "I don't do commitment" was what I said. And I said it like I was imparting some profound insight. Truth be told, his question struck me as absurd. I hadn't yet realized that I dealt in absurdity like Facebook dealt in friends. It was my constant companion.

. . . .

*I was arrogant, self-indulgent, selfishly ambitious,
impatient, and instinctively rebellious.*

. . . .

I was a project. But slowly I began to see I was God's project. The gospel was "bearing fruit and growing" in my life, as Paul says in Colossians 1:6. As I allowed God's Word to abide in my life, I began to live more and more like a disciple in John 15 fashion. Holiness toward God began to matter to me. Loving God and loving others became an increasing preoccupation. Maybe most significantly, I just wanted to know the Savior, to learn how to worship him with my life.

Strong Stirrings

But there were other stirrings—vague and formless at first, but potent enough to press questions upon my mind. They first took shape in the local church I was "attending." Somehow I ended my sojourn, came into camp, and actually joined the church. And I really liked it! I started not just attending meetings and spouting opinions, but connecting with brothers and sisters and catching a vision to build life together. Older guys began to speak into my life, helping me see the wretch in me and the grace in others. I started to grow as a Christian. And I began to serve in the church—doing little things, unnoticeable things, because that's all they trusted me with. And I liked that too—which freaked me out. I started to realize that what I brought to the game didn't really matter, but what we did together built things that last.

The stirrings, the vague questions, kept coming up in my mind. It was freaky. A church planter or pastor would step up to the pulpit to preach God's Word. Across the room I could hear the rustling of Bibles and the muffled sounds of people preparing to listen. Some leaned forward, eager for a choice helping from Scripture. Others were almost fearful, opening their Bibles with a desperate sense of need for God. Still others sat back, ready to rate the preaching, enjoy a story, or laugh at a clever joke. But something different was happening in me. Watching the preaching drama unfold, I was thinking: *How does he do that*?

Now you may respond, "Every person who's ever heard a decent sermon has asked that question." But this was different. This wasn't theoretical. It was personal. Watching men in ministry ably function in their gifts caused me to mentally project myself into their place. I had dreams of marinating in God's Word so that I too could stand and deliver the results. In fact, I used to practice preaching when I was alone or out in the woods. You know, just to give voice to things about God that were stirring in my soul. There were no woodland conversions, but it fed a desire to preach God's Word.

. . . .

This wasn't theoretical. It was personal.

. . . .

And these experiences began to poke at a deeper question, a question of calling, a question that inched into my personal space: *Am I called to do that?*

Where's a guy supposed to go with that? I didn't know where to start. Was the answer found in some knock-you-to-the-ground Damascus Road experience? Hey, I was wide open to seeing the Lord and chatting about my future. In fact, as long as I had his attention I might add other agenda items to the conversation. But that never came for me. In fact, over my twenty-six years of ministry, I've discovered it doesn't come that way for most men.

How do you know if you're called to plant a church or be a pastor? I remember a church member who sat across from his pastor testifying that he'd received "a call to ministry." He went on with no little verbosity, informing his pastor of how humbled he was to receive the call and how awed he was to be chosen. Never asked a question, never invited any evaluation.

Then he informed the pastor he would be leaving the church in search of his ministry. So is that what happens? God speaks so loudly to a man that the others' voices become unnecessary?

I wondered if getting into ministry was like applying for a job—you know, matching qualifications with the right opportunity. If someone's good with teens and great on his feet, and there's a need for a youth worker, then presto! You got the job! Qualifications plus need equals ministry, right?

And then there was the question of Bible college or seminary. Those schools exist to confirm a man's call and get him into ministry, correct? Well, that wasn't a live option for me. You see, I had more issues. I had one called "college-debt-and-no-daddy-trust-fund-to-pay-it." I had another called "forgot-to-think-about-the-future-because-I-was-having-too-much-fun-in-school." And I had a third issue called "I-met-this-great-Christian-girl-and-we-want-to-get-married-NOW!" Those three issues combined to deliver me into the wacky world of being a security guard. In my book, that wasn't exactly Pauline preparation for ministry.

And I was still left with the stirrings, with a desire to be in ministry. What was the next step? How did I know if God was calling me to be a pastor?

A Weighty Adventure

God answered those questions for me. I want to tell you more about my journey in the following chapters, because this book is my answer to those questions. Those questions are important, and they're not unique to me. They may be essential to your future. I hope you keep reading.

Perhaps your exploration has moved you from curiosity to earnestness to all-out desperation. Believe me, I hear you. This process is an adventure—one that gets pretty serious and requires desperate prayer. Charles Spurgeon thought so as well: "How may a young man know whether he's called or not? That's a weighty enquiry, and I desire to treat it most solemnly. O for divine guidance in so doing!"[1] That's the kind of appropriate sobriety and divine dependence worth locking down as we begin this journey.

If you're looking for entertainment, you're going to be disappointed. Yes, I want this book to engage and inspire you, but we must never lose sight of the weight of this inquiry. The summons of a man into pastoral ministry has always been treated as a solemn thing. The people of God depend on the right man leading them in the right way. So I want to provide answers to the real questions you have as you ponder pastoral ministry.

Along the way I have several goals. First, as you read this book, I want you to connect your call to ministry to something far greater: the identity you have in Christ. As John Piper has said so well, "Brothers, we are not professionals." So many men have gone into Christian ministry and lost who they are as Christian men. I'm glad God relentlessly came after my heart (and does to this day) rather than shooting me through an impersonal ecclesiological pipeline. I want to help you be who you are in Christ as you respond to the call to serve him.

Another of my goals is to set the call to pastoral ministry in the context of a glorious vision for the church. The pastoral ministry, and therefore the pastoral call, doesn't exist apart from its expression in a biblically defined local church. I'm glad

God ruined me with a love for the church. I want to help you see that you need the church as much as the church needs you.

. . . .

I want you to connect your call to
ministry to something far greater.

. . . .

I also want to help you diagnose your call through the biblical requirements for God's shepherds, right up front.[2] There are many ways a guy can set himself apart in people's minds—personality, political savvy, brains, selfish ambition. But God's Word is surprisingly specific about what it takes to lead his people. I'm grateful the Bible hems me in as a pastor. I want to offer you six simple questions that should be answered by every man who feels called to ministry.

I want to help you not only do the hard work of self-evaluation, but also prepare for daily evaluation from others. Ministry can be a lonely and frustrating experience. We need others in our lives to help us get there and stay there. I'm so glad God placed men around me from the beginning who have helped confirm, define, and support my call. I want to help you embrace what it means to have your call confirmed.

Finally, I hope this book teaches you how to prepare. You'll see there isn't a magic highway into ministry. Often the road is not of our own choosing. Sometimes we're not even sure we're going in the right direction. I'm so glad I can look back and see how the Lord used all my experiences as preparation; and he's still doing that today. I want to help every man in this process learn how to wait in faith and prepare in wisdom.

Excited yet?

Spurgeon had it right: it's weighty stuff. Not simply because it involves our personal future—it's way bigger than that! This is weighty because it involves the proclamation and protection of the gospel. It's weighty because it calls for care for God's people. It's weighty because this world needs strong churches planted and built for the glory of God.

Are you being summoned? Before we can consider our call, we need to consider the One who calls. That's the best place to begin our journey.

Before each of the remaining chapters in this book, you'll see short profiles like the following. Each man profiled is a hero of the faith. Together, they're a diverse group, representing a variety of religious traditions. Some were formally trained for the ministry; others acquired their doctrine through rigorous self-training. Some were known for preaching, others for leadership, others for wisdom, others for sacrifice. I hope you'll find a kindred spirit among them. But it's what these men have in common that's most important. First and foremost, they all loved the gospel and the doctrines of grace. Not only was each man unswerving in his commitment to the gospel, but he also made it the cornerstone of his ministry call. Second, all of them walked out their call in local church ministry.[3] While theologically astute, none made their mark in the world of academia. While mission-minded, none traveled the world starting new works. And while renowned preachers, all wrote and spoke first for the local congregation to whom they were committed. In short, they were pastors—first-rank pastors to be sure, but local church men just the same. Most served only one primary church for their entire ministry lives; their ministry tenures to their primary local churches averaged more than thirty years. All these men have passed on into glory; their race is done, and now we can consider the full fruit of their responses to God's summons to ministry as a stimulus to our own faith.

For Additional Study

The Cross and Christian Ministry, D. A. Carson
Biblical Eldership, Alexander Strauch
Lectures to My Students, Charles H. Spurgeon

A Summons Story
Thomas Scott: Called to Conversion[1]

It started with a chance meeting at a dinner party . . . and an ambitious young minister looking to make a name for himself. There's nothing like taking on one of the old guard in a battle of theological wits to burnish the reputation. So began the providential relationship between Thomas Scott and the venerable John Newton in May 1775.

Thomas Scott was one of the bright young lions of the Anglican Church in the eighteenth century. Well-educated and a gifted communicator, Scott had one little problem: he didn't believe the gospel. He had new ideas he wanted to share.

Seizing the opportunity of the dinner party encounter, Reverend Scott asked Newton if he could write him to seek advice on some weighty spiritual matters. Newton, ever looking to inspire younger men in gospel ministry, was happy to oblige. But this wasn't a mentorship; Scott intended to trap Newton.

In his own words, Scott gives his strategy:

> Professing friendship and a desire to know the truth, I wrote him a long letter, really wishing to provoke a discussion of our religious differences. . . . I did not care for his company. I did not mean to make any use of him as an instructor, and I was unwilling the world should think us in any way connected. I used every effort to draw Mr. Newton into controversy, disputed almost everything he advanced, and was much nettled at many things he asserted.

But John Newton was well aware of Scott's intentions. Newton's letters of response carefully answered baiting questions with biblical truth while avoiding the hooks to engage in speculative theology. More significantly, Newton made it his point to press the gospel at every turn. Frustrated with his lack of results, Scott gave up. But God began to expose the shaky hypocrisy Scott had built not only his ministry on, but also his life.

He writes of having occasion to call on Newton

> under discouraging circumstances . . . and his discourse so comforted and edified me, that my heart, being by his means relieved from its burden, became susceptible of affection for him. From that time I was inwardly pleased to have him for my friend . . . I had, however, even at that time, no thoughts of learning doctrinal truth from him, and was ashamed to be detected in his company.

But the seeds of the gospel had begun to take root in the heart of Scott, and at some point in the year following their first meeting, Scott the curate became Scott the Christian. Newton was astounded.

Hearing him preach in the first months of Scott's gospel ministry, Newton exclaimed,

> My heart rejoiced and wondered. O my Lord, what a teacher art Thou! How soon clearly and solidly is he established in the knowledge and experience of Thy gospel, who but lately was a disputer against every point! I praise Thee for him. . . . Now he seems enlightened in the most important parts of the gospel and will I trust prove an instrument of usefulness in Thy hand.

Newton's trust was well founded. Thomas Scott, converted minister, became one of the shining lights in the eighteenth-century Evangelical Awakening. He put his prodigious intellect to work, writing the most acclaimed Bible commentary of the time. He became a cofounder of missionary and Bible distribution works that thrive to this day. And Scott became pastor of the most influential church in London during the second half of the century.

It was during his time at Lock Chapel that Newton sent a young, spiritually confused man to hear Scott. The man wasn't unlike the young Thomas Scott—brilliant, ambitious, and spiritually confused. Newton was discipling him, but knew he needed to sit under the ministry of a truly gifted preacher. And it was under Scott's weekly gospel preaching that young William Wilberforce would be established in the faith that eventually led him to take on the evil of slavery.

2

Summoned
to the Savior

· · · · · · · · · · · · · · · ·

Phone calls always had a strange, peace-shattering, life-giving power for my young kids. Whether sleeping, playing in another room, or listening to music with the decibel level set on "rock concert," a single ring from a phone would catalyze them into action and catapult them toward the source. Collisions were common, though no emergency room visits came of it. How come? More sophisticated minds may not get it, but to them, unlocking the mystery of the caller was as suspenseful as a Hitchcock thriller. Who knew what fun might be unleashed, what travel might result, what intrigues might await? It could be Gandalf recruiting for an adventure, or pirates needing ship-mates, or maybe even the president looking to field-test some ideas with the prepubescent set. The right call could alter their entire evening—maybe their entire destiny.

Or maybe we just needed to get out more.

In any case, my kids detected something important: calls come from callers. A ringing phone is proof positive that someone from outside has turned his or her attention toward us. My wise and insightful children realized early on that they couldn't conjure up a call. No amount of concentration or wishful thinking can induce a phone to ring. The caller's initiative is everything.

· · · · · · · · · · · · · · · ·

The caller's initiative is everything.

· · · · · · · · · · · · · · · ·

This is why it's unfortunate that this whole business of calling so often begins in the wrong place, with the wrong question.

Dude, let me ask you a question. Do you think I'm called?

This is a great question, an awesome and mysterious question. Scripture would add that it's a noble question. I can say from my own experience that it's a seriously exhilarating question. But I also want to state from the outset that it's not the most important question. Guys asking this question are often looking hard at their résumés, reckoning that the bottom line is their education, character, competence, or experience. It typically starts with who they are or what they're destined to do. But that approach just doesn't seem to line up with Scripture.

Now I don't want to be picky, but I've learned something. There's another, more magnificent place to start: God. The call to ministry is about God's character and activity, about his mercy and love, and ultimately about his provision to those for whom he died. If the Caller's initiative is everything, then we must preoccupy ourselves with the Ultimate Caller.[1] It's that simple—and that profound.

God at the Bottom of It All

Pastor and theologian Sinclair Ferguson has pointed out that "one of the New Testament's most frequent one-word descriptions of the Christian is that he is 'called.'"[2] Which makes us wonder: What are we supposed to do with that?

Seems like we've got two options. We can imagine it makes much of us: God called *me!* Or we can see it as making much of God: *God* called me!

Who's really at the center of the Caller's call?

I know a guy who knows people, if you know what I mean. This guy told me about a trip he once took when he picked up a flu bug. Too sick even to get out of bed, he spent three days stuck in a hotel room. In the middle of the second night, his phone rang. I would have ignored it, but he picked it up. Get this: the president of the United States was on the line. My friend (I've decided anybody I know who knows the leader of the free world is automatically my friend) had once done some work for the president. The president somehow heard he was sick, and called to inquire about his health. My friend told me he jumped out of bed and stood at attention in his boxers to continue the conversation.

As this guy related his story to me, it was evident this call was one of his life's highlights. And that wasn't because of him. It was because of the caller.

In an infinitely more profound way, our call to ministry, just like our call to salvation, ultimately says little about us and a great deal about the Caller.

If we're truly to understand the importance of calling in ministry, we need to grasp that the impetus for it originates with a wise, loving, and sovereign God. And before he calls us to ministry, he calls us to himself.

· · · · · · · · · · · · · · · · ·

Before he calls us to ministry, he calls us to himself.

· · · · · · · · · · · · · · · · ·

This Caller has "called us to a holy calling" (2 Tim. 1:9). Our self-understanding as believers is fundamentally wrapped up in the wonder of this frequently repeated truth:

> God is faithful, by whom you were *called* into the fellowship of his Son, Jesus Christ our Lord. (1 Cor. 1:9)

> And those whom he predestined he also *called*, and those whom he called he also justified, and those whom he justified he also glorified. (Rom. 8:30)

> We ought always to give thanks to God for you, brothers beloved by the Lord, because God chose you as the firstfruits to be saved, through sanctification by the Spirit and belief in the truth. To this he *called* you through our gospel, so that you may obtain the glory of our Lord Jesus Christ. (2 Thess. 2:13–14)

As you can see, the calling spoken of here is not a summons to vocational ministry, but something much more profound and fundamental—what theologians refer to as the *effective* (or *effectual*) *call*. Wayne Grudem defines it as "an act of God the Father, speaking through the human proclamation of the gospel, in which he summons people to himself in such a way that they respond in saving faith."[3] This calling is *from* God (Eph. 1:3–6; 4:4–6) and calls us *to* God (Rom. 1:6–7). In other words, the call for our salvation precedes and grounds all other callings.

This is the point that John Newton's friend, Thomas Scott, finally got. He'd accepted a call to ministry, but he had no confidence in a call from God. Newton was right to lock in on this. He was willing to be ridiculed because he knew that a man over God's people who doesn't know God is like the *Titanic* putting to sea—a tragedy in the making.

If we understand the gospel correctly, we see several important things about this call to salvation:

The Caller is pursuing his enemies—those who never wanted to hear his voice (Rom. 5:10; Col. 1:21). He isn't pursuing his friends or peers in this world, because there aren't any.

The Caller visited earth in person. The gospel summons came not as an audible voice or angelic vision, but in a personal visitation, the incarnation of the Lord Jesus Christ. "The Word became flesh and dwelt among us" (John 1:14).

Through the cross, the Caller restored the lines of communication and fellowship that had been severed by sin. We don't discover the call of God by modeling his example or emulating his teachings. Jesus came ultimately to yield his life on the cross in ransom for ours. Through his atoning blood, our connection to the Caller is finally established. By that connection our hearts are made new, our eyes and ears are opened, and we can hear and heed the ongoing callings of God.

The gospel is the instrument of our call. The gospel—the good news of Jesus Christ—is the instrument by which God issues his effective call to us and brings us into new life and union with Christ by grace (Eph. 2:5). It's a call *out of* something: the bondage and blindness of sin. And it's a call *into* something: renewed fellowship with the God who created us.

When we cut to the chase, we realize that the One who calls has done it all.

Charles Spurgeon discovered this prior call in a memorable manner one evening when he was "sitting in the house of God":

> The thought struck me, *How did you come to be a Christian?* I sought the Lord. *But how did you come to seek the Lord?* The truth flashed across my mind in a moment—I should not have sought him unless there had been some previous influence in my mind to make me seek him. *I prayed*, thought I, but then I asked myself, *How came I to pray?* I was induced to pray by reading the Scriptures. *How came I to read the Scriptures?* I did read them, but what led me to do so? Then, in a moment, I saw that God was at the bottom of it all, and that he was the Author of my faith, and so the whole doctrine of grace opened up to me, and from that doctrine I have not departed to this day, and I desire to make this my constant confession, "I ascribe my change wholly to God."[4]

What Spurgeon grasped and held on to through years of fruitful ministry was that before we do, God has done. In everything, God is "at the bottom of it all!"

Getting a Grip on the Gospel

"Okay," you might be saying, "I got it, Dave. My soteriology's locked down. But I'm looking to move beyond that—I want a role where I can help others get what I've got."

But that's the trap. We assume the gospel, and then dedicate ourselves more to the special call of ministry. We stop reading books about the atonement and start reading books on leadership. We want to be relevant, so we study culture more than the cross. There's no growth metric we can't cite, no new church models we're not familiar with, no leadership trends we aren't tracking.

Here's the irony: those called to preach the gospel can be the most susceptible to drift from the gospel. That's why it's vital for the man pondering a call to ministry to have a firm and sustained grip on the gospel. Edmund Clowney's words on this are just as relevant for the church planter as they are for the pastor celebrating a silver anniversary in ministry:

> There is no call to the ministry that is not first a call to Christ. You dare not lift your hands to place God's name in blessing on his people until you have first clasped them in penitent petition for his saving grace. Until you have done that the issue you face is not really your call to the ministry. It is your call to Christ.[5]

. . . .

Considering a call to ministry can be like slashing through a jungle overgrown with questions.

. . . .

Your question of calling isn't merely subsequent to the call to Christ; it's essentially tied to it. In fact, it's only because our primary call is secured through the gospel by the cross that we can rejoice in exploring a ministry call.

Getting a firm and tightening grip on the gospel clears the mental path to more helpfully ponder your call. Considering a call to ministry can be like slashing through a jungle overgrown with questions—big, hairy questions like: *Who am I? What if*

I wash out as a pastor? Do I have what it takes? What should my priorities be? The gospel cuts through the overgrowth and ensures we're thinking about ourselves and our ministry rightly. It stirs faith, nurtures hope, and helps us hear the Caller clearly. Let's look at some of the answers the gospel brings to those big hairy questions, and why they're important.

The Gospel Supplies My Identity

Imagine being called to ministry by none other than Jesus himself—in person. It happened to Paul that way. He was marching to Damascus as a hired gun with Christians in his crosshairs, when Christ appeared with news of a career change. Paul was to become "a chosen instrument of mine to carry my name before the Gentiles and kings and the children of Israel" (Acts 9:15). A call to global ministry from the risen Christ would tend to become an identity marker, don't you think? After all, a supernatural call is a brilliant branding strategy.

There's no question Paul's call was unique and essential to his ministry. But what fundamentally defined him was neither what he was called to do, nor his education or social standing, nor his career or background. Knowing Christ as Lord surpassed everything: "Indeed, I count everything as loss because of the surpassing worth of knowing Christ Jesus my Lord" (Phil. 3:8).

Being chosen for ministry is great. Being chosen for sonship is infinitely greater. Who am I? I'm one with Christ, no matter what happens with any specific sense of calling I may have. My union with him is the most important and meaningful thing about me. Keeping this as our source of identity is essential.

Don't believe me? Just talk to a man who's had to step out of ministry. Maybe a church can't afford to keep him. Perhaps his health is an issue. Or maybe he's under discipline. It doesn't matter. A man finds out where he truly locates his identity when he can no longer do the ministry he felt called to do. We should all live with our resignation letters on our desks. If during transition time my fingers have to be pried off my ministry, something went colossally wrong. That's why I need to keep my grip on the gospel. It supplies my main identity.

The Gospel Is Adequate—I'm Not

There's a guy I want to speak to just now. He's the one who thinks God might be calling him to be a pastor, but he's scared stiff about it. He wonders if he can cut it. Maybe he's making a good salary and doesn't want to take the financial hit. Or he's seen leaders crash and burn in moral failure. Whatever the reason, he's looking for a place to hide—as if God will see his reluctance and move on to the next unsuspecting victim . . . uh, candidate.

I can relate. During those years when I was wrestling over whether I was called to ministry, I was the head of security for a major department store. One time I had to tussle a guy to the ground because he was stealing clothes from the store. It wasn't my most pastoral moment. He got bloody, the cops came, reports were taken.

A few days later I had a strong impression that I was unqualified for pastoral ministry because I was a man of bloodshed. That may sound nuts to you, but when you're an impressionable young security guard hoping to become a pastor, strange thoughts can speak pretty loudly. Fortunately, a pastor got hold of me and set me straight. "Dave," he said, "you're an idiot." Good pastors know just what to say, and that's what I needed. But I'll never forget feeling unqualified, unworthy, too stained for what Paul called "a noble task" (1 Tim. 3:1).

. . . .

I'll never forget feeling unqualified, unworthy,
too stained for what Paul called "a noble task."

. . . .

Maybe that's how you're thinking. Well, buddy, here's what the gospel says: we're not perfect—we're not even capable—but God loves to use human inability as an earthly canvas to display his glory. We see this in our salvation, where God supplied everything except the sin from which we're saved. "For by grace you have been saved through faith. And this is not your own doing; it is the gift of God, not a result of works, so that no one may boast" (Eph. 2:8–9). When we have a grip on the gospel, grace turns our eyes away from our fears and weaknesses and places them on God. We're actually able to hear the pastoral call because of the gospel.

But it doesn't stop there. Ministry trepidation exists because you expect a bad outcome—you're afraid you'll do something wrong or fail in some spectacular fashion because of your inadequacy. It's true that you're unworthy, incapable, and filled with potential failures. But here's the good news: acknowledging those limitations is what makes you a fit vessel and starts you on the path of fruitful service. God designs gospel ministry in a manner that diminishes us and exalts him. "God chose what is foolish in the world to shame the wise; God chose what is weak in the world to shame the strong . . . so that no human being might boast in the presence of God" (1 Cor. 1:27, 29).

Don't treat your fears and weaknesses as if they're some strange phenomenon previously unknown in the annals of Christian history. God arranges ministry so it flows from weakness. He appoints the least likely to have the greatest impact. Maybe your apprehension is just a sign that you're getting the point.

The Gospel Sets My Priorities

Does your sense of call orbit around your own abilities, vision, or performance? The gospel call says infinitely more about the glory and grace of God than it does about those things. When a man is called by God to ministry, he does well to remember that both his salvation and his service come from God and are aimed at returning us to God. As Os Guinness reminds us, "First and foremost we are called to Someone (God), not to something (such as motherhood, politics, or teaching) or to somewhere (such as the inner city or Outer Mongolia)."[6]

Our salvation isn't simply a contractual arrangement where we form a partnership to achieve certain goals. God's call carries his design and intention—specifically, to join us into a love relationship with himself through his Son in which we're growing in intimacy with, knowledge of, and conformity to Jesus. This will always, day in and day out, remain our primary and most important calling. And it's this relationship with God—not our intellect, competencies, or gifts—that will always position us best to serve God's people most effectively. God's reconciling work positions us to engage God and his Word and then supply others with what we read, hear, and experience. All other calls bow to this one.

Once after a church service where I preached, I was cornered by someone who was considering membership. The young man asked, "What can you tell me about your devotional life?" My first thought—*well, from your question, apparently it doesn't help my preaching*—remained wisely stifled as I commended his inquiry. Somehow this insightful listener had come to discern something many believers never grasp: few things could summarize my relationship with God quicker than a brief rundown of my devotional life. And to this chap, my active, fervent relationship with God mattered.

A lot of guys look at pastoral ministry as a blissful mixture of study and sweet communion with God. And it is, if you can find time between meetings, counseling, phone calls, administration, hospital visits . . . a seemingly endless list. There's a reason why it's important to build "consistent devotional life" into every pastor's job description. It's just as hard for a pastor to die to himself and live as if he really needs God as it is for a politician, computer programmer, or police officer. But pastors keep God at the center in public when they're pursuing him passionately in private.

The Gospel Is What Really Matters

I just read a story in a news journal last week. It seems a brother and sister in London were cleaning their parents' home when they found an old vase. They were tickled over the quaint relic, set it aside, and eventually turned it over to an auction house for sale. There they discovered it was valued at almost $2 million.

But get this. In the auction, spirited bidding drove the price up to $69.5 million. Their relic turned out to be an eighteenth-century Qing dynasty vase. I have no idea what that means, but it always seems as though anything with "dynasty" in its name immediately becomes expensive. The comment from the auction spokeswoman really caught my eye. She said the brother and sister "had no idea" what they'd found, and when the final bid was official, they "had to go out of the room and have a breath of fresh air."[7]

Christians are like that. We discover something valuable in the gospel—precious enough to save us—but we don't recognize its true worth. Like the brother and sister, we possess it but don't perceive it. What was said of them could be said of many believers: we have no idea what we have.

God raises up leaders to ensure the gospel is preached, applied, and valued in the daily life of the church. The purpose of ministry proceeds from and orbits around the prized *evangelion*, the gospel. Remove the gospel, and authentic biblical ministry disappears.

Think about it this way: if there were no gospel, no saving work of Jesus Christ, would there be a need for pastors? Apparently so, if you drive around any town in America and see the amount of churches and other religious buildings filled with things that have nothing to do with Jesus Christ. Or drop in on religious classes at any number of denominationally affiliated universities, and you can make a pretty good case that if we junk the gospel, pastors still have plenty of work to do.

• • • • • • • • • • • • • • • •

Remove the gospel, and authentic biblical ministry disappears.

• • • • • • • • • • • • • • • •

Truth is, gentlemen, if we don't have a gospel, we don't have a job—at least as God sees it (1 Cor. 2:2). We exist because God's people need men to gather them into local families and preach to them the Word of God in faith and power. Sure, they need to talk about their problems, have people officiate their marriages and funerals, and participate in wholesome family-friendly activities. But all that could happen without pastors. Men are called as church planters, as pastors, to celebrate the worth of Jesus Christ—to make sure it's never said of their congregation in regard to the gospel, "They have no idea what they have."

Brothers, if you love the idea of pastoral ministry because you think you're qualified to help people with their problems, or because you can ponder theology, or because you like the idea of people coming every week to hear the latest thing you have to say, then serve the church by getting off the bus. Pastoral ministry exists for the proclamation and protection of the gospel for people inside and outside the church. We need to value the gospel and know what we have so we can share it with others.

John Bunyan sat in jail for twelve years rather than allowing the gospel to be censored in his preaching. His thinking was,

Why be a free pastor if I can't preach the gospel? It was clear to Bunyan: removing the gospel made pastoral ministry irrelevant. Is it clear to you? Do you know what you have?

Is the Gospel Enough?

Are you wondering when you'll get off the bench and into the big game? Do you realize that the works of ministry (loving God and others, witnessing, serving in the local church, discipleship, etc.) are all expressions of the work of the cross in our lives, not of a specific ministry call?

As a believer, you *already* have a full-time ministry: to bear fruit as a disciple of Jesus Christ (John 15:1–16). In the rest of this book I want to stoke a passion for pastoral ministry. But whether you ever hear that summons to shepherd God's people, you've already heard the gospel—the most important thing that will ever be said to you. And you've heard it from the Caller himself.

Is that good enough for you?

For Additional Study

The Cross of Christ, John R. W. Stott

What Is the Gospel?, Greg Gilbert

Pierced for Our Transgressions, Steve Jeffery, Michael Ovey, and Andrew Sach

Seeing and Savoring Jesus Christ, John Piper

A Summons Story
Charles Simeon: Called to the Church[1]

What if somebody gave you a church but didn't let you in? This was the predicament Charles Simeon faced. It was his first pastorate. At age twenty he'd converted to Christ on Easter Sunday. Now twenty-three, he was appointed vicar of Holy Trinity Church in Cambridge.

This wasn't just a job; it was the fulfillment of a dream. "I had often—when passing Trinity Church, which stands in the heart of Cambridge—said within myself, 'How should I rejoice if God were to give me that church, that I might preach the Gospel there and be a herald for Him in the University.'" And now he was installed to lead the most prominent church in the middle of a university that educated the best and brightest in England.

But Simeon soon realized he wasn't getting the red carpet treatment. A sizeable faction in the congregation, including many key leaders, had another guy in mind for the job. In Simeon's Anglican world, the ecclesiological organization had the right to install pastors and control the Sunday services. But the local church wardens controlled the facility. Enter the awkward standoff. Simeon couldn't be barred from preaching at the Sunday service, but the wardens could lock the pew boxes, effectively removing all the space for people to sit.

The wardens kept the pastor locked out of the building the rest of the week. So Simeon's ministry consisted of preaching to as many people as could fit in the aisles of the church on Sunday mornings, and meeting with as many folks as he could fit in his tiny apartment during the week. This pretty much sums up the first ten years of Simeon's pastorate at Holy Trinity.

Pastor Simeon was caught between the proverbial rock and a hard place. He was assigned to this congregation by the denomination that had ordained him. He believed he was called not just to a church, but *this* church, and he wanted to be faithful. But he also loved the church and didn't want to create a showdown with the opposition that would damage the flock. That simply couldn't happen. So, Simeon chose to serve the interests of the church by humbling himself.

> In this state of things I saw no remedy but faith and patience. The passage of Scripture that subdued and controlled my mind was this, "The servant of the Lord must not strive." It was painful indeed to see the church, with the exception of the aisles, almost forsaken, but I thought that if God would only give a double blessing to the congregation that did attend, there would be on the whole as much good as if the congregation were doubled and the blessing limited to only half the amount. This comforted me many, many times, when, without such a reflection, I should have sunk under my burden.[2]

Simeon endured. He refused to exercise rights as a minister if they would give reason to split the church. Why?

To understand Simeon's perseverance, you have to understand Simeon was a church man; he knew that no man had the right to mold God's church to fit his needs. But he lived with an abiding sense of responsibility to God for this church. While Simeon could have gone elsewhere, he chose to stay and be counted a failure.

And so he stayed. For life.

Over time, God changed the church. The hearts of some were softened, the influence of others diminished. Simeon eventually led the church and was there for fifty-four years. Holy Trinity Church kept him as their pastor till the day he died.

In the church sanctuary, there's an inscription in his honor:

In Memory of
the Rev. Charles Simeon, M.A.
senior fellow of Kings College,
and fifty-four years vicar of this parish, who,
whether as the ground of his own hopes,
or as
the subject of all his ministrations,
determined
to know nothing but
Jesus Christ and him crucified.
1 CORINTHIANS 2:2

3

The Context
of the Call

· · · · · · · · · · · · · · · ·

Imagine yourself in Charles Simeon's shoes. It's your first pastoral assignment, and on day one there's a sign tacked on the door saying your services are no longer needed. Man, that's a tough church. Speaking for myself, people typically need to hear me preach at least once before they say that. But Simeon didn't even get that far. He was locked out, cut off, and shut down. And since Starbucks wasn't around, there were few options for a side job. What's a newly minted pastor to do?

Today we have options. Can anyone say, "Back to school"? Grab a loan, start a PhD, pitch a tent in the library. Or there's always sales—you know, agree on a commission rate and live the life of faith. Or you could open a counseling office. Maybe start your own blog, or take all that entrepreneurial drive and launch a ministry. But how many of us would seriously consider the Simeon way? I mean, why bother?

Charles Simeon understood something too easily overlooked today: the Caller connects the call to the church. At first glance that might seem about as obvious as the "Danger: Steep

Hill" signs at the Grand Canyon. But for many men, the call doesn't quite make it to the church. They envision themselves preaching for the glory of God—you know, Bible open, arms outstretched, voice set on "spiritual"—and transforming people's lives through wise teaching and counsel. But they don't give much thought to where that's supposed to happen. They feel called into this mysterious thing called "ministry," but strangely, not called into the church.

The Bible, however, doesn't talk about *what we do* as the context of our call. It talks about *where we do it*. First Peter 5:2 calls pastors to "shepherd the flock of God that is among you, exercising oversight." Acts 20:28 calls pastors to "pay careful attention to yourselves and to all the flock, in which the Holy Spirit has made you overseers, to care for the church of God." The local church is the essential context for pastoral ministry. This means *if you're called to pastoral ministry, you're called to the church.*

Simeon didn't hit the eject button and spring himself from the church. Neither should we. The church is God's visible people, his body on the earth. And the call to pastoral ministry belongs there.

Training: The "Where" Matters

When a passion for the church is added to a grounding in the gospel, a proper understanding of ministry calling begins to form. If you believe you're called to pastoral ministry, you must see your potential calling *in the context of the local church*, where ministry is shaped and defined according to Scripture.

This makes sense. But think about it for a second. You

might be in a church right now but considering hitting the road to get training somewhere else—seminary, Bible college, parachurch ministry. Funny thing about us evangelicals: we take men who are *in* the church *out of* the church in order to send them *back into* the church to do ministry *for* the church. Is anybody else confused?

Suppose you had a guy whose greatest dream was to make doughnuts. He couldn't imagine a life where he wasn't covered with flour and sugar, helping out in the little shop where he grew up. A dream stirs in his heart—he wants to make doughnuts for these folks the rest of his life. So what do we do with Doughnut Joe?

If we follow the common model for training pastors, we tell him he's got to leave the doughnut shop and go to doughnut school—study the history of doughnut making, parse the intricacies of recipe texts, be able to cogently argue the merits of traditional doughnut design versus the modern fat-free varieties. You get the idea. Joe becomes a "professional" now. But that path takes him far away from the neighborhood shop where he's always dreamed of carrying out his vision.

Somehow we reached the point where the most commonly accepted approach to training pastors is to draw gifted men away from the local church and educate them largely outside it. Don't get me wrong—this isn't about seminary bashing. I went to a great seminary while serving my local church. It gave me a deep appreciation for the key role that Christian educational institutions play in helping the church protect sound doctrine and train teachers and scholars for the advance of the gospel.

But there are other important aspects to training men for

ministry, areas where the Bible school or seminary can often bump up against limitations. I'm thinking specifically of identifying called men, evaluating their call, assessing their character, and positioning them to be fruitful in their call. That's the responsibility of the local church.

Not long ago, I participated in a roundtable discussion with the leaders of a seminary about the many pastors who leave ministry, whether through discouragement or disqualification. These leaders were engaged in some thoughtful institutional soul-searching about their effectiveness in preparing men for the long-term trials of ministry. I was there primarily as a learner. The discussion eventually centered on the fact that at this seminary, as at a great many others, the admissions process was inattentive to the calling or character of the applicants. These leaders had my sympathy. Their institution was essentially training men who had committed to study for pastoral ministry, but without a sound assessment of their pastoral call. This is an institutional limitation, and it's why the local church must remain on the point for evaluating calling and character.

· · · · · · · · · · · · · · · ·

Identifying called men . . . is the
responsibility of the local church.

· · · · · · · · · · · · · · · ·

Here's another limitation of seminary: if we're not careful, we treat the ministry like a skill set that can be memorized, drilled, tested, and graded—all in isolation from the people we want to serve. Take medicine, for example. I'm glad my doctor went to med school. I'm glad that before he started working on live people he was cutting up dead ones. I'm really glad he's been trained to know the difference between a benign and a malignant tumor, and that he can talk about things I could probably never understand. I'm really glad he didn't just say one day, "I'm going to learn me some medicine," then immediately start doing appendectomies on my friends.

But pastoral ministry isn't like medicine. Soul surgery can't be practiced on dead people. And all of our book knowledge doesn't amount to much if we can't make it relatable to other people. An ability to parse Greek is commendable, but it's of little help as a pastor if you can't apply the gospel to someone's life. No wonder a report on pastoral transitions gives this sobering snapshot:

> Studies indicate that a pastor does not reach significant effectiveness until five to seven years into a pastorate. Some observers suggest ten years. When we consider that the average pastorate lasts from three to seven years we see that we have a problem. The question is; what is the problem?[1]

Guess what? Yours truly has an opinion on that (one that's shared by many, including a number of leaders at Bible schools and seminaries). I suggest the problem arises when a guy enters the ministry with no prior training in a local church. He's got no experience in soul surgery.

Pastoral ministry is ministry among God's people. So why do we think we can train a guy best by extracting him from the very people he's supposed to serve? If you're wondering whether you're summoned to the ministry, think carefully about where you'll practice caring for souls.

If You're Called to Be a Pastor, You're Called to Love the Church

Here's one more thing to remember if you're pondering your calling and downloading application forms. Seminaries will never be able to impart a love for the local church in future pastors unless they labor in partnership with the local church. Commendably, many seminaries make this their aim. But they would be the first to admit it's difficult to achieve. Kentucky pastor Brian Croft observes,

> How sad and all-too-common it is for a young man to spend years in seminary and be cut off from any local-church involvement! Then he graduates and somehow he thinks that a love for the local church will magically come with the salary he accepts from his first pastorate. Yet a love for the local church is displayed by a commitment to it, realizing that it is the means through which God primarily is building his kingdom and accomplishing his purposes in the world.[2]

In *The Reformed Pastor*, a classic exposition of Acts 20:28, Puritan divine Richard Baxter says that without "the proper public spirit towards the Church" no man is fit to be Christ's minister. And he describes such a spirit in these words:

> He needs to delight in its beauty, long for its happiness, seek for its good, and rejoice in its welfare. He must be willing to spend and to be spent for the sake of the Church.[3]

That's pretty radical stuff, and it didn't come naturally to Richard Baxter any more than it will for you or me. He acquired this delight from seeing it in the apostle Paul, who told the church in Corinth, "I will most gladly spend and be spent for your souls" (2 Cor. 12:15).

What place does the local church hold in your sense of call? Where do you see it in relation to your ministry future? As essential? Optional? Irrelevant? Is a local church, to you, more than just a logical place to send your résumé? What does your present involvement with the local church say about your biblical priorities? Is the church, in your eyes, where you want "to spend and be spent?"

Let's face it. If you're called to pastoral ministry, you're being called to the local church. It's where we move from being donut lovers to donut makers. Is the donut shop in your plan?

How to Love the Church

Okay, Dave, I hear what you're saying. I got it. Local church equals priority. But how do I do that? I've gotta get training somewhere, right?

Let me offer you a couple of steps to start with. And I'll throw in some street-level observations on why I think the pastoral call is often decoupled from the local church context—while giving you some concrete ways to fight that tendency.

Be Ambitious

Think about it. If you're going to plant a church or become a pastor, you must aspire to the call. But aspiring to that kind of thing gets uncomfortable. Not to mention it's easily misunderstood by others. How come? It seems like Christians have an awkward relationship with ambition. We really don't know what to do with it. But here's what we need to see. When Paul wants to kick-start the conversation on how to identify a man called to eldership, the first evidence he offers is rooted in ambition: "If anyone *aspires* to the office of overseer, he desires a noble task" (1 Tim. 3:1).

A man truly called to pastoral ministry will pulse with a legitimate, God-ordained aspiration. In fact, Paul indicates that somehow he'll make that aspiration known. How would Timothy know a man's desires unless the man said something about it?

God doesn't want the church to be so careful about the possibility of selfish ambition that we neglect to stoke godly ambition. There's much to say on this topic. If you're interested, I've written a book on it—*Rescuing Ambition*. But if you've already vowed this is the last Dave Harvey book you'll ever read, hear this: a man who's ambitious for pastoral ministry either has been seriously dealt with by God, or is about to be seriously dealt with by God. If that's you, get ready for some serious (and sometimes dangerous) grace.

· · · · · · · · · · · · · · · ·

A man truly called to pastoral ministry will pulse with a legitimate, God-ordained aspiration.

· · · · · · · · · · · · · · · ·

And if I may have a word with pastors: it's clear in 1 Timothy 3:1 that Timothy is supposed to be looking for men who aspire to eldership—and not cut them off at the knees because they're a threat to his ministry. He's making a way for their call, for their ambition. Trust me: God has a way of slapping selfish ambition silly when it appears in called men—for their own good and the good of the church. So when you meet a man aspiring to pastoral ministry, don't cut him down. Whisper a prayer for him. There may be an invisible hand swinging for him. More importantly, you may well be seeing a sign of the summons.

Aim for Service, Not Career

There's nothing wrong with careers. Plenty of young men need to find one. To be career-minded assumes a certain degree of business mastery, self-interest, personal reward, and public recognition—and a "career" becomes the delivery system for those goals. I'm not saying these things are evil. In fact, for civilizations to develop and for industry and commerce to thrive, these things need to be encouraged.

But here's what I'm saying. *The church is not a career path.* It's a place you go to give your life away. God's people can't be mere stepping stones to larger opportunities. They're a primary focal point for the entire enterprise of calling.

Let's face it. Seminaries offer street cred—professional accreditation for a ministry role. The problem is not the seminaries, though, because they're providing a theological education, and they accomplish that goal. The problem is the called man and his heart. The church suffers when called men crave careers and potential pastors chase professional distinction.

In his clarion call to pastors aptly titled, *Brothers, We Are Not Professionals*, John Piper says,

> The professionalization of the ministry is a constant threat to the offense of the gospel. It is a threat to the profoundly spiritual nature of our work. I have seen it often: the love of professionalism (parity among the world's professionals) kills a man's belief that he is sent by God to save people from hell and to make them Christ-exalting, spiritual aliens in the world.[4]

Here's something else. When the church chases professional qualifications, we create a ministry elite. We mistakenly train people to trust credentials, not character or competence. David Wells calls the craving for professional gravitas "The D-Min-ization of Ministry." He writes, "Insecure ministers who are stripped of importance hope to be elevated through professionalization to the same social standing as other professionals, such as physicians and lawyers."[5]

· · · · · · · · · · · · · · · · ·

When pastors stalk prominence,
ministry becomes endangered.

· · · · · · · · · · · · · · · · ·

Now, in the interest of full disclosure, I've got a DMin (though it hasn't helped my social standing one bit over at our Acme). But I think Wells is talking about more than community clout. He means that when pastors stalk prominence, ministry becomes endangered.

God calls all pastors to study, and some pastors to higher education. The history of the church is filled with great pastors who never received formal ministry training—maybe you're familiar with names like Newton, Spurgeon, Tozer, and Lloyd-

Jones. It's also filled with top-notch scholars, men who earned academic accolades but never pointed to their credentials for validation of their call.

The eminent theologian John Owen (who earned two degrees at Oxford) was enthralled with the uneducated John Bunyan, who was his contemporary. When this came up in conversation with King Charles II, the king expressed amazement that so learned a man as Owen could sit and listen to an "illiterate tinker" such as Bunyan. Owen's response? "May it please your Majesty, I would gladly give up all of my learning if I could preach like that tinker."[6] That says a lot about Bunyan's informal education. It also shows that Owen was far more than a theology wonk. He understood that clear gospel preaching was essential, while formal education was not.

In case you're now prepared to take your high school diploma and start knocking on church doors looking for work, hold on. There are a couple of important things you need to hear.

First, I'll just say it: you're probably not much like Newton, Spurgeon, Tozer, or Bunyan. Rather you're probably more like I was—an ordinary guy wrestling through an extraordinary call and wondering where the whole thing leads. It may indeed lead you into some formal academic study of the Bible. Don't ever despise scholarship. The church will falter without people skilled in Hebrew, Greek, Aramaic, and other languages necessary for hermeneutical clarity and integrity.

Second, please monitor your heart for the church as you expand your mind in the academy. If they're not complementing each other by moving you toward the church in exploring and positioning for your call, something's wrong. When the seminary fails to prepare men for ministry in the local church, the seminary diminishes in impact and relevance.

The gospel is not a message detached from a people; it creates a people. And when the local church occupies a prominent place in our hearts, we'll be positioned to serve those people and not merely advance our own ambitions.

Pastors, Raise Up Pastors!

Let me talk again to pastors for a second. A lot of young, gifted men come to the sad conclusion there just isn't any place for them in their churches to launch into their calls. Want to help with the youth? Absolutely. Lead a small group? Plenty of needs? Jump in. Be a deacon or a missionary? Sign on! But to be a church planter or pastor? Sorry, buddy, all slots are filled, but there's a good Bible school down the road.

Check out the biblical requirements for planting a church, which, by the way, are the same requirements for pastoring a church. Notice how the vast majority of them involve character. The local church is the obvious place where such requirements can be cultivated and assessed. Sure, seminaries can impart knowledge, but they're just not set up to deal with character. Character evaluation requires the local church. Pastors, that requires you.

No church can or should hire gifted guys just to keep them in the church, but every church or family of churches should have a strategy for developing and deploying its own pastors. Paul's words to Timothy are pretty amazing: "And what you have heard from me in the presence of many witnesses entrust to faithful men who will be able to teach others also" (2 Tim. 2:2). There are actually four generations of doctrinal transfer represented in this command—from Paul to Timothy, then from Timothy to faithful men, then from the faithful men who transmit it to others. It's remarkable, God's strategic plan for gospel-transfer. And it's entrusted not only to Timothy, but to pastors of local churches as well.

It's a nonnegotiable: churches need to train pastors as an investment into the future. Seminaries can supplement, but they never replace the local church. If we don't identify and train called men, we'll lose them.

Al Mohler, who leads one of today's most prolific evangelical seminaries in America,[7] has this to say:

> I emphatically believe that the best and most proper place for the education and preparation of pastors is in the local church. We should be ashamed that churches fail miserably in their responsibility to train future pastors. Established pastors should be ashamed if they are not pouring themselves into the lives of young men whom God has called into the teaching and leadership ministry of the church.

Where Is the Church in Your Call?

Take a deep breath, because in the next section of this book, we're going to dive deeply into how you can know you're called. But everything we'll talk about presupposes that your sense of call is focused more on serving the church than on fulfilling a dream.

Here are some questions you should think about now, because they're going to make a big difference later.

- What's your present involvement in a local church? If you were a pastor, would you be any more committed to the church than you already are? What does your answer say about you?
- If you were offered a position serving your present church as a pastor, would you take it? Why or why not?
- If you were asked to take the pastorate at a church where you didn't know anybody and nobody knew you, what would influence your decision to take it or not?
- Under what circumstances could you see yourself leaving a church you were shepherding?
- What is your church's or denomination's accepted practice of training and deploying pastors? Where do you agree with this practice? Where do you have questions about it?
- If you were asked by a church you were pastoring to step down in favor of another man leading the church, would you look for another church to pastor, or would you remain at the church as a faithful member? What would determine your next move?

The bottom line: The Caller loves the church. The Caller created the church. The Caller guarantees the effectiveness of the church and promises that the church will prevail. The Caller died for the church. The Caller provides leaders for the church. And the Caller calls men into that leadership through the church itself. Therefore we must determine from the outset that in whatever ministry direction we're heading, we're summoned to "spend and be spent" for the sake of the church.

For Additional Study
Why We Love the Church, Kevin DeYoung and Ted Kluck
Nine Marks of a Healthy Church, Mark Dever

A Summons Story
Lemuel Haynes: Called to Godliness[1]

Character matters for every pastor. But for some, character is the thread of credibility that will determine whether a call will be fulfilled or denied. For Lemuel Haynes, ministry was about character.

Haynes is a marvel of God's providence in the formation of character in a gospel minister. Born in New England in the 1750s, he was a first-generation black slave in colonial America. Abandoned as an infant by his parents, he was taken in by a white Christian family, whose indentured servant he became until the age of twenty-one. In their home, Haynes was taught the ways of the Lord and the sound doctrine of Edwards, Whitefield, and other Calvinist evangelicals. He matured at the outbreak of the Revolutionary War, where he served gallantly as a Minuteman and a regular army soldier until he was mustered out due to illness.

Due to his prodigious intellect, Haynes was offered a scholarship to Dartmouth College to train for the ministry. But he chose instead to train in the trenches of ministry with local church pastors. In 1785, he was ordained into pastoral ministry as a Congregational minister, the first African-American ever formally called into ministry. His first experience in church leadership came as part of a group planting a church in Massachusetts.

Early on, opportunities for Haynes to step into pastoral ministry were limited by racial prejudice, despite his evident character, confirmed call, and preaching gift. But in 1788 he received a call from a small congregation of forty-two people requesting his service in Rutland, Vermont. There he served as pastor of an all-white church for thirty-three years. During his tenure the church grew to 350 people and had a strong gospel-proclaiming presence in New England.

In 1818, both Haynes and the congregation reached the conclusion that his long season of ministry in the Rutland church had ended. Upon departing, he continued in faithful pastoral ministry, serving two more churches over the next fifteen years, finally retiring from the ministry due to deteriorating health. All told, Lemuel Haynes devoted forty-eight years to local church pastoral ministry.

Perhaps the greatest legacy of his ministry is his fidelity to godly character. Surely one reason for this is the pressure he faced as a black man seeking to minister in a white world that accepted racial prejudice as a way of life. As a patriarch of African-American ministers, he carried the burden of being "above reproach" in a way that few men can comprehend. But in the end, this doesn't appear to be the driving reason for his conscious emphasis on godliness. His greatest concern was for the glory of Christ and the way that pastors, in particular, are called to uphold it in the world. One biographer said this about him: "Haynes well understood that the bar of Christ, especially for a minister, would be a time of penetrating judgment, a time at which the heart and habits of the pastor would be laid bare and his just rewards be made known."[2]

Any man considering a call to pastoral ministry must submit to the test of his character. And he would do well to heed the words and proven example of Haynes:

> Above all, the great God with approval or disapproval beholds the transactions of this day; he sees what motives govern you and will proclaim them before the assembled universe. Oh solemn and

affecting thought! The work before you is great and requires great searching of heart, great self-diffidence [caution] and self-abasement. How necessary that you feel your dependence on God; you cannot perform any part of your work without his help. Under a sense of weakness go to Him for help. . . .

Although the work is too great for you, yet let such considerations as these revive your desponding heart. Because the cause is good, better than life, you may well give up all for it. . . . The campaign is short and your warfare will soon be accomplished; the reward is great, and being found faithful, you will receive a crown of glory that fades not away.[3]

PART TWO

Diagnosing the Call

. . . .

4

Are You Godly?

· · · · · · · · · · · · · · · ·

Was that a voice? Samuel heard something, but he wasn't sure, and it wasn't clear. Was it his dinner talking back, or maybe just a dream? No, it sounded like a voice. He ran to Eli saying, "Here I am, for you called me" (1 Sam. 3:5). Perplexed, Eli marched him back to bed.

It happened a second time. Heaven opened, God called, Samuel woke. Once again, off to Eli.

Given Eli's reputation in the Bible, I must indulge certain embellishments. I picture him sunk deep in an overstuffed chair, a TV clicker in one hand, day-old Chinese food in the other. He's wearing a faded and well-stained T-shirt purchased years before at one of the more raucous temple concerts he attended with his two sons. Wiping moo shu from his mouth, he waves off Samuel, saying, "Yo, kid, take an Ambien and stop bothering me" (1 Sam. 3:6, my translation). Samuel shuts the door and lies alone in silence, anticipating something yet hearing nothing, all at the same time.

God calls a third time. Samuel returns to Eli—fortunately during a commercial. Just as he's about to send Samuel back to bed, an inspired thought takes root. Eli "perceived that the LORD was calling the young man" (1 Sam. 3:8). Eli mutes the infomercial and tells Samuel that the next time he hears the call, he's to say, "Speak, LORD, for your servant hears" (1 Sam. 3:9).

Samuel returns to bed. The unrelenting Caller speaks a fourth time. This time Samuel hears . . . *him!* God's word became connected to God's man. A ministry began.

Samuel was called, but he couldn't hear. Most men wrestling through these issues can identify with him. We hear what seems like a calling—our circumstances speak, our desires speak, other people speak. But how do we know when a call is from God? Samuel didn't know. Eli didn't know, at least not at first. How can we be sure?

The next section of this book is dedicated to exploring how you can be sure. We'll explore six questions, the answers to which can reveal a genuine call to plant or lead a church. We're going to spend a ton of time in the Pastoral Epistles, because that's where called men should spend a lot of their time.

In fact, let me suggest an exercise right now. Just set this book down, get to a Bible, and read 1 Timothy 3 and Titus 1.[1] Then come back. These aren't the only passages we'll look at in this chapter, but they're the ones we're starting with. We've got some exciting stuff ahead.

Can Anyone Live Up to This?

Okay, you back? Good. Those passages outline Scripture's requirements[2] for eldership. And it's in these passages that we find the first question to ask when it comes to exploring a call to ministry: *Are you godly?*

I want to start by making a couple of essential points about this question. If you're like most guys, the lists of qualities in 1 Timothy and Titus seem far out of reach, like you might as well nominate yourself for Supreme Court justice. ("No, Senator, I don't really know anything about the law, but I think a job you can't be fired from is something I'd be great at.") Upon first glance, we're looking in these passages at blow-the-average-guy-out-of-the-water standards for pastoral ministry. I mean almost apostolic!

So here are two things to consider. First, the majority of these qualities are actually commanded of all believers in some fashion. To be "sober-minded, self-controlled, respectable, hospitable," to be "not a drunkard, not violent but gentle, not quarrelsome, not a lover of money," and to manage well one's household, "with all dignity keeping his children submissive" (1 Tim. 3:2–4)—no Christian is sprung from those. It's not like pastors and elders can't get drunk while believers are free to chug beer like frat boys. No, most of these apply to all Christians. Still, I understand—it's a little unsettling to see them assembled in one place staring you down like an offended cage fighter on game day.

But here's my point. The man called to ministry is not some kind of super-Christian who lives by a higher code. Nope, he's just a called man with gifts that enable him to lead God's people and with a grace that empowers him to be an example. "The minister today," says Joel Nederhood, "is really nothing more than an ordinary member of the church of Jesus Christ, who is called to express His nature as 'man of God' in an especially high degree."[3]

Here's another thing. Called men can approach these passages like an unbending standard that demands conformity and punishes disobedience. This happened to Freddie. He was amped to give his life to the church in ministry. Then somebody dropped the requirements of Timothy and Titus on him like a pro wrestling move. Flopping around on the hard canvas of crushed aspirations, Freddie looked for a tap out. A nice sales job came along, and boom, he was outta the ring and counting cash. Freddie's still very involved in his church, but he's haunted by the feeling that maybe he wasn't supposed to get out of the fight that easily. What "mighta been" never really goes away.

· · · · · · · · · · · · · · · ·

*God's call upon a man delivers the grace
necessary for the godliness needed.*

· · · · · · · · · · · · · · · ·

If that's you, don't miss the wonderful news contained in these passages. It's the glorious discovery of *prior grace*. God's call upon a man delivers the grace necessary for the godliness needed.

This point can deliver some serious "aha," so let me unpack it a bit more. In 1 Timothy 3 and Titus 1 we see extraordinary evidences of God's activity that *precedes* any clear sense of calling. Think again of Paul's use of the present-tense controlling verb "must be" in 1 Timothy 3:2. The elder must be above reproach, sober-minded, self-controlled, respectable, etc. This verb tense carries throughout the passage.[4] Paul isn't holding out a list of character goals yet to be achieved. He's speaking of qualities already present. They're preconditions for the elder, not outcomes eventually hoped for.

So what does that mean? Just this. Paul indicates there's grace at work in certain men to produce a certain kind of life. Timothy will know called men because grace is already active to create godliness. Identifying a called man isn't about interviewing candidates or reviewing their GPAs; rather, it's a glorious exercise of discovering a deposit of empowering grace. Grace shines through their lives and becomes a sign that they're summoned to pastoral ministry.

Indeed, no man can be an example of 1 Timothy 3 and Titus 1 unless prior grace is coursing through his soul. "Sincere grace," said Jonathan Edwards, "is a powerful principle in the soul, and the power of it appears partly in the nature of its actings. It is no dull, inactive, ineffectual thing. There is a holy ardency and vigor in the actings of grace."[5]

. . . .

"God's work in a man demonstrates God's call of a man."

. . . .

Keep in mind, we'll never see these qualities perfected in anyone. But while not *perfected*, they should be evident, and will be in any man who's called to ministry. My friend Jeff Purswell, the dean of the Sovereign Grace Pastors' College, puts it simply: "God's work in a man demonstrates God's call of a man."[6]

This also means that to appoint pastors with the hope that before too long they'll somehow rise to Scripture's eldership standards is both shortsighted and extremely dangerous. It's like asking somebody to land a fighter jet because they've flown one in a video game. Men don't become pastors because of potential. They become pastors because God's grace is already at work in them.

So can anyone live up to these requirements for ministry? Yes, because God's call delivers grace! His summons is never barren; it bears grace to accomplish the purpose of the call. The Caller bids us come and then empowers us to get there. If you're called, you can stand confident that God has already begun working in you (see Mark 3:13). God's standards are not burdensome; they're actually a magnificent confirmation of his sovereign purpose for the called man's life. God's grace produces a godly life—and that godly life helps confirm God's call.

Let's get more specific on what godliness really means.

A Called Man Is Converted, and Sure of It

"He must not be a recent convert" (1 Tim. 3:6). Breaking that down, let's start with the blatantly obvious: the called man must be a *convert*. Yep, we're plunging the depths now, aren't we? Pastors must be Christians—*truly Solomon-like stuff here, Dave.*

But implicit in this requirement is that the man has been road tested. His maturity and humility have weathered some miles and are proven reliable. That's why those words are followed with "or he may become puffed up with conceit." Paul wanted Timothy to understand that appointing immature men to ministry becomes a dangerous journey.

Here again we see that the gospel must be the orienting

reality of our lives. If a man doesn't have the gospel right and square when he enters ministry, his trials and temptations can overturn everything. We're not just talking about an experience of salvation here. We're talking about a theology of salvation as well. There can be no discussion of calling or pastoral ministry apart from biblical conversion—the effectual calling of God to salvation in Jesus Christ through trust in the gospel.

But there's another facet of this as well. There's no true godliness apart from conversion. Conversion, as the word implies, is an exchange. In soteriology (salvation theology), it's a conversion from old life to new life. In conversion, old cravings are replaced with new ones. Conversion creates affections for God and desires to be godly. It's the beginning of God-pleasing, Spirit-generated, lasting change. The new birth, as John Piper says, "is Jesus' root remedy for our depravity. Personal and social and global renewal will not be possible without this most fundamental of all changes. It's the root of all true and lasting change."[7]

You can be an unconverted religious professional. But to be a pastor, you must be converted. And the called man should not be a "recent" convert, Paul says. This "not recent" criterion is curiously, but purposefully, undefined. Paul refuses any pressure to assign a minimum age or "years-in-Christ" requirement for the man called to lead in the local church—thereby helping us avoid legalistic interpretations. For a group of new believers, a four-year-old Christian may be the statured sage. And this is often what happens in areas where the gospel is breaking out in fresh ways. But the more mature a congregation becomes, the more maturity it needs from its leaders.

Either way, the reason for the "not recent" criterion is clear.

Character, gifting, and competencies are essential, and like fine wine, they require time to become well aged in the local church. The goal isn't simply to spare the congregation upon whom he is inflicted. It's a protective mechanism for the called man, so that he doesn't "become puffed up with conceit and fall into the condemnation of the devil" (1 Tim. 3:6). That's the last thing a pastor needs.

A Called Man Has Godly Character

In his excellent book *Biblical Eldership*, Alexander Strauch makes the following insightful comment: "God provides objective, observable qualifications to test the subjective desire of all who seek the office of overseer. Desire alone is not enough; it must be matched by good character and spiritual capability."[8]

Good character. Here's how that's portrayed in Timothy and Titus (and notice the obvious priority God places on it). The called man must be:

- holy and above reproach (1 Tim. 3:2, 8; Titus 1:6, 7)
- the husband of one wife (1 Tim. 3:2; Titus 1:6)
- sober-minded and self-controlled (1 Tim. 3:2; Titus 1:6)
- respectable and well thought of by outsiders (1 Tim. 3:2, 7)
- hospitable (1 Tim. 3:2; Titus 1:8)
- able to teach sound doctrine and refute those who oppose it, holding to the trustworthy word as taught (1 Tim. 3:2, 9; Titus 1:9)
- not given to drunkenness (1 Tim. 3:3, 8; Titus 1:7)
- gentle, not violent or quarrelsome (1 Tim. 3:3; Titus 1:7)
- not arrogant or overbearing (Titus 1:7)
- not a lover of money or pursuing dishonest gain (1 Tim. 3:3, 8; Titus 1:7)

- managing his family well, with obedient children who are believers and not open to the charge of debauchery or insubordination (1 Tim. 3:4–5; Titus 1:6)
- not a recent convert (1 Tim. 3:6)
- a lover of good (Titus 1:8)
- disciplined (1 Tim. 3:8)

Why is it necessary to spell out particular character requirements for pastors? Because God is wise, and he knows what's best for the church and for the men who lead it. These detailed character requirements protect the integrity of the preaching office of the church (James 3:1). A pastor represents Christ before the world and the church. He sets the standard of maturity and conduct in the church—a standard that must be "above reproach" (1 Tim. 3:2; Titus 1:6). By guarding his life and doctrine (1 Tim. 4:16), he maintains the credibility of both.

Another reason for these character requirements is that the temptations of indwelling sin, particularly selfish ambition and pride, can be a particularly strong and consistent challenge for leaders. The call to godliness protects pastors and moves them toward humility. Pastors don't have handlers. They don't have PR staffs. But, reputation matters. To be a pastor is to be a self-acknowledged sinner representing a holy God. A pastor makes it his aim to pursue godliness because his life is a vessel of the message he is called to preach. And if you realize the value and glory of the message—and the One whom the message is about—you'll realize that humility is the only appropriate approach to a life called to proclaim it.

Character requirements ensure that a man can take it when things get hot in the leadership seat. Pastoring is a taxing and often discouraging labor, and should not be thrust upon a man who's unprepared or undeveloped. These passages in Timothy and Titus clarify the character that absorbs the cost of the call.

And there's a flip side. As one writer aptly notes, the Bible "says more about what a leader is to be than it does about what he is to do. . . . If he does not meet requirements of biblical morality, he is unfit to be a leader in God's church."[9]

· · · · · · · · · · · · · · · · ·

Too often, when a man's character hasn't stood the test, he remains in ministry by simply rewriting the test.

· · · · · · · · · · · · · · · · ·

Too often a man is set aside from ministry because of church politics or vague assessments of deficiencies. And too often, when a man's character hasn't stood the test, he remains in ministry by simply rewriting the test, making it about his popularity or prior service. But Scripture provides clear, evaluative categories that focus on the observable fruit for a guy pursuing ministry. These categories greatly serve both the man and the church. The church is assured that favoritism or power struggles will not define the evaluation of a man in ministry. The man is assured that he'll be measured by clear, biblical criteria.

"Ministry is a character profession," pastor Charles Swindoll says. He continues:

> To put it bluntly, you can sleep around and still be a good brain surgeon. You can cheat on your mate and have little trouble continuing to practice law. Apparently, it is no problem to stay in politics and plagiarize. But you cannot do those things as

a Christian or as a minister and continue enjoying the Lord's blessing. You must do right in order to have true integrity. If you can't come to terms with evil or break habits that continue to bring reproach to the name of Christ, please, do the Lord (and us in ministry) a favor and resign.[10]

Among all the biblical requirements for the called man, gospel-empowered character seems to be most prominent. A man's character is the overarching scriptural qualification for leadership in the church—and this will be revealed in everything from the nuance of his word choices to the cravings behind his big decisions. Amazingly, these requirements also illustrate the depth of God's love. It's almost as if God is saying, "Only the highest godliness is eligible to tend my dearest possession—my people!"

A Called Man Is a Servant

You know him. He works one day a week, plays golf the other six. When you call, he's always "in his study"—which can sometimes be code for wasting time. He sees himself as an extemporaneous preacher—meaning, he gets up on Sunday and talks about whatever drops into his head. Where he's really good is in the offering slot. That's where you see the passion and the power. That's where the man does his best work.

Who is he? Well, he's not any pastor I know. But he's the pastor that many folks in our culture assume fills every pulpit and leads every church. Somehow the average person never gets to see what a pastor really does. They never get to see him serve. I remember a guest greeting me after a Sunday message I preached and inquiring what I did for a job during the week.

Maybe that was his way of saying, "Now that I've heard you preach, don't quit your day job."

Let me drop you in on a little pastoral training seminar. In Mark 10 we find Jesus and the Twelve disciples on their way to Jerusalem—for the last time. Jesus leaves no doubt that the reason he's going there is to die. The twelve don't get it (do they ever?). When James and John start a boneheaded argument about who's going to be great, Jesus gently levels them, and then the other ten pile on. If I were Jesus, I'd drop-kick the whole bunch at this point. But Jesus doesn't, because school's in session and he wants to teach them something important about life after he's gone:

> And Jesus called them to him and said to them, "You know that those who are considered rulers of the Gentiles lord it over them, and their great ones exercise authority over them. But it shall not be so among you. But whoever would be great among you must be your servant, and whoever would be first among you must be slave of all. For even the Son of Man came not to be served but to serve, and to give his life as a ransom for many." (Mark 10:42–45)

We tend to look at this as instruction for all Christians, which it is. But it's instruction specifically for the leaders of God's church. Note the contrast: rulers of the Gentiles contrasted with the future leaders of the church. One set lords it over people; the other serves the people.

And just to make sure we don't lock this back in the apostolic age, in verse 45 Jesus universalizes it—he came to serve "many." So this call to serve, specifically the call upon leaders of Christ's church to see themselves as servants, comes to every aspiring pastor, because it comes from the Chief Pastor himself.

• • • • • • • • • • • • • • • •

This call to serve . . . comes to every aspiring pastor . . . from the Chief Pastor himself.

• • • • • • • • • • • • • • • •

A pastor is a Christian specifically summoned to serve God's people in the ministry of teaching, leadership, and oversight. This identity is essential to his calling. It keeps him from assuming that his leadership begins with his rights or preferences.

Consider the following perspective from D. A. Carson:

As someone who has taught seminary students for more than 15 years, I worry about the rising number of seminarians who, when asked where and how they think they might best serve, respond with something like this: "Well, I think I would like to teach somewhere. Every time I have taught, people have told me I have done a pretty good job. I get a tremendous sense of fulfillment out of teaching the Bible. I think I could be satisfied teaching Scripture."

How pathetic. I know pagans who find satisfaction and fulfillment by teaching nuclear physics. In any Christian view of life, self-fulfillment must never be permitted to become the controlling issue. The issue is service, the service of real people. The question is "How can I be most useful?" not "How can I feel most useful?"[11]

Dr. Carson has invested much of his life in training men for the ministry. His perspective should sober us all. Often we say we want to serve God, when the way we live reveals that we expect him to serve us.

What is the antidote for self-serving ministry? *To live as a servant of Christ.*

So what does the call to service mean for the summoned man?

- The summoned man works where there is need, not just where he can express his gifts.
- The summoned man works to make those above him a success, not to develop his own success.
- The summoned man is just as happy to use service to address his weaknesses as to hone his strengths.
- The summoned man seeks to make the work of those around him a joy.
- The summoned man uses his influence to promote the church's good, not his own advancement.
- The summoned man works with excellence, diligence, and faithfulness for the attention of Christ, not others.
- The summoned man walks boldly on the path of sacrifice and treads cautiously on the path of promotion.
- The summoned man joyfully steps back in order to let another man step forward.

If this conversation about service is rocking your view of calling, don't be discouraged. Nobody who has ever really pastored God's people has been exempt from the call of servanthood. And trust me, you won't be an exception.

Be a Model of Your Message

There's a final implication to all these requirements listed by Paul: the pastor is called to model his message. His leadership is authenticated through character. The pastor leads through his life as well as his lips.

The epitome of this model is (as always) Jesus Christ, the incarnated Word of God. Christ didn't simply offer powerful preaching, but modeled the veracity of his words through his actions. His life validated the truth he spoke.

Pastors are called to follow in Christ's footsteps by being examples to the flock (1 Pet. 5:3) and becoming living examples of the realities they teach. Grace kindles a fire to cultivate a life that images the Caller and his message. Without the life behind the voice, their message rings hollow and the Caller's image is distorted. The called leader doesn't simply regurgitate biblical truths; rather, he talks about Scripture through how he applies it.

· · · · · · · · · · · · · · · ·

It takes both a man's message and his example to mature a church.

· · · · · · · · · · · · · · · ·

The reality is that it takes both a man's message and his example to mature a church. Jesus gave the principle like this: "A disciple is not above his teacher, but everyone when he is fully trained will be like his teacher" (Luke 6:40). For the man aspiring to the ministry, this means the leader typically represents the high-water maturity mark among the people of the church. His strengths will become their strengths, his weaknesses their weaknesses. As John MacArthur observed, "Whatever the leaders are, the people will become."[12]

I'm so grateful to God for the pastoral team at my church. They're men of whom this world is unworthy, modeling godliness in a manner that provokes me. They're not just caregivers; they're standard-bearers for me and others. I want to be like them when I grow up.

I can't think of a better way to end this chapter than to give Robert Murray McCheyne's perspective. His words inspire and convict me at the same time; they summarize what the character requirements of ministry are all about: *"The greatest need of my people is my personal holiness."*

That's why the church, by God's grace, will wisely ask this question about every man who's potentially called by God to ministry: *Is he godly?*

For Additional Study
The Godly Man's Picture, Thomas Watson
Humility: True Greatness, C. J. Mahaney
Charity and Its Fruits, Jonathan Edwards
Holiness, J. C. Ryle

A Summons Story
Martin Luther: Modeling the Pastoral Home[1]

They call it the fishbowl effect—the awareness that everything you do is being watched by someone else. It's not paranoia, because it's true. You're being watched.

Perhaps no man in history had more experience with the fishbowl effect than Martin Luther. The priest had started out looking for an argument, but found himself the center of the Reformation. All eyes were on him. The Catholic hierarchy was looking for him to slip up, to do something that would discredit him; his followers looked to him to show them how to break traditions going back a thousand years. And the world watched, waiting to see what would happen.

So Luther had to go do something totally outside the box. He had to start a family. Now remember, for over a millennia, being a minister—pastor, priest, monk—required a celibate life. And here was Luther rewriting the moral code. What's more, he married *a nun!*

Why he married isn't easy to fathom. Though he declared the abomination of requiring a celibate clergy, yet he earlier made it clear marriage wasn't for him. Now here he was, a forty-one-year-old former priest, marrying Katharina Von Bora, a renegade nun sixteen years his junior. Publically, the best Luther could muster for his pursuit of marriage was that his father was hounding him to do it. But those who looked closer saw a man who, in his own awkward way, had wooed a formidable woman who would be the helpmate on his treacherous journey.

Throughout their marriage of twenty years, the Luthers were supremely conscious of two things. First, they were carving out a model of the pastoral home that others would follow, for good or ill. People were watching. And they embraced the entire family vision—having six children and creating a household that included several needy relatives and countless short-term boarders. The Luther home was not a quiet place.

So what did people see when they looked at the Luther marriage and family? They saw union—two becoming one. Though the personalities and gifts of Martin and Katherina were markedly different, God used the marriage to sanctify each of them and create a union that became dear as the years progressed.

One author summarized the value of the Luthers' example this way: "The success of any marriage depends on two people who aren't afraid to grow and change as Martin and Kate did"[2]—and who aren't afraid to do that changing before the eyes of the whole world. The reluctant groom was changed to the point where he was ultimately brought to say, "There is no more lovely, friendly, and charming relationship, communion, or company than a good marriage."[3]

In the Luthers, people saw family vision. Their decision to have children was radical in itself, and not just because of the constant threat on Luther's life. It was commonly understood at the time that if a priest and a nun were to ever bear a child with one another, the result would be a two-headed monster.[4] Instead, Luther found in his family a joy that he never imagined. He devoted himself to raising his "little heathens" to see their need for the Savior, but also brought them into his tender care.

He did, however, find parenting to be more of a riddle than the thorniest theological issue. As he once noted, "Christ said we must become as little children to enter the kingdom of heaven. Dear God, this is too much! Have we got to become such idiots?"[5] But Luther's ultimate assessment of parenting is far more visionary: "No power on earth is so noble and so great as that of parents."[6]

If any pastor wonders if it's fair to have his family life be part of the evaluation of his call, let him remember Martin Luther. This patriarch of the pastor's family has left a great example of faith and family fidelity.

5

How's Your Home?

······················

Helping men sort through their calling is best done over Chinese food. It's hardly a Pauline principle, but I discovered years ago that men talk more openly about their dreams when stuffed to the rafters with beef and broccoli. (Don't knock it if you haven't tried it!)

From a church planting recruitment standpoint, the guy eating sweet-and-sour chicken across the table from me that day was quite the candidate. He was seminary trained, experienced in ministry, connected into evangelical circles around our city, and hungry to preach. He was the proverbial quarterback still on the bench. I was hoping to put him on the field calling plays.

Then he mentioned in passing that he and his wife attended different churches. To him it seemed incidental. To me, a flag had just been thrown, and the play needed to undergo review. Inquiring about the church his wife attended, I discovered that her church taught foundational doctrines contradictory to the ones he believed. He said this troubled him. Yeah, it troubled me too.

When he asked for the next step toward ministry, I

mentioned that any assessment of his calling would involve an exploration of this apparent dichotomy in his home. I suggested that it would probably begin with what his wife's choice of churches revealed about his leadership in his family.

I haven't seen him since.

The Everyday Evidence

It's a common mistake among those who feel called to plant and pastor churches: some men are willing to lead the church before they lead their families. In fact, some guys seem willing to lead the church to the detriment of their families! Both options are unacceptable to God. He poses a question that offers no multiple choice answers: "For if someone does not know how to manage his own household, how will he care for God's church?" (1 Tim. 3:5).

Remember 1 Timothy 3 and Titus 1? One of the most striking things about the biblical qualifications for pastors is Scripture's assumption that the home reveals and validates the leader.[1] Paul is crystal clear on this:

- "the husband of one wife" (1 Tim. 3:2; Titus 1:6)
- "hospitable" (1 Tim. 3:2; Titus 1:8)
- "he must manage his own household well, with all dignity keeping his children submissive" (1 Tim. 3:4)
- "his children are believers and not open to the charge of debauchery or insubordination" (Titus 1:6)

And it's no secret that many of the other requirements Paul mentions will be tested and revealed—repeatedly and inescapably—at home:

- "self-controlled" (1 Tim. 3:2; Titus 1:8)
- "able to teach" (1 Tim. 3:2)
- "not . . . arrogant or quick-tempered" (Titus 1:7)
- "upright, holy, and disciplined" (Titus 1:8)

Even a scan of Paul's lists shows that the quickest way to determine whether a man is qualified to lead a church is to take a reading on how effectively he leads his wife and children. If he leads well, their voices will rise to confirm his call and testify to his credibility. If he leads poorly, they'll shadow his candidacy with gnawing questions and contradictory messages.

A Word to Single Men

Okay, single guys, listen up. I imagine you sitting there ready to bail on this chapter, maybe even on your call to ministry, because we're now talking about home life and you have neither a wife nor kids. I'll spare you the customary comments to single guys—Jesus was single, Paul was single, etc.—to make a couple of points that may be more helpful to you in this process.

. . . .

Your call will make a claim upon your wife and family.

. . . .

The overwhelming majority of men in ministry will be married, and that probably includes you. So it's best to know that your call will make a claim upon your wife and family. When you come aboard the good ship *Ministry*, tickets are also issued for your future wife and kids. You sail together on this journey. Make sure any girl you're sweet on knows about the vessel. She doesn't need an independent call to sail, but she does need to know that she is marrying a man on a journey. She should be prepared to say, "Where you go I will go, and where you lodge I will lodge. Your people shall be my people, and your God my God" (Ruth 1:16).

But here's something else you don't want to miss. I want you to see this chapter not as a call to rush out and get married, but as a call to live under a biblical leadership principle that should inform the rest of your life: y*ou will lead from who you are in private.* Right now that may be living with roommates or with parents. In the future it will be with a wife and probably kids. But you must learn to live and lead from the inside out. As John Kitchen says, "The life you live in private determines the ministry you can have in public."[2]

The Leadership Lab

Think about it. Why do you think Scripture directs our attention to the home? Two reasons jump to mind.

The Hardest Place to Live the Christian Life

I know the military has its unique challenges, the political life offers untold temptations, and corporate careers carry daily trials for Christians. But I'm sticking with this proposition: *the home is the hardest place to live the Christian life.* It's one of a kind.

Just think about it. There's no other place where high expectations (love your wife as Christ loved the church) meet a desire to be unplugged. There's no other setting where a strategic role (father) meets distraction from that role (entertainment). There's no other venue where the human heart is unscreened—people encounter the real you. Show me another place where all this stuff happens 24/7, and I'll make sure I never move there.

But there's something else. The home offers the largest window on whether you meet Scripture's character requirements for ministry. In that sense, the home is essential to assessing calling. I think that's because God knows something we often miss. You can pose at the office or play religious at church, but your family knows and reveals the true measure of the man.

. . . .

In the home, nobody's impressed with accomplishments, rank, or income.

. . . .

My home gets Dave in the raw, unedited version. My daughter told me the other day that she met someone who referred to me as an author. She told me she never thought of me that way, which is proof positive that she's actually read stuff I've written. But I think she also meant that she doesn't see me first through the roles I play outside the home such as pastor, speaker, or writer. You see, in the home, nobody's impressed with accomplishments, rank, or income. To her I'm just Dad, fellow saint, fellow sinner, the guy down the hall who greets her each morning, prays for her at night, and can never find his keys.

Yeah, there are times we all wish our families lived with our bios under their pillows. But that would be artificial, because what we've done *out there* isn't usually who we are at home.

Our families see us in the routine of life, battling bad habits, walking through conflict, trusting God for finances—who we really are. It's the unvarnished experience of real life that makes the home such a hard place to live out what we believe. But it also forms a great window into our leadership. John MacArthur knows the Bible, and pastors, and he knows this issue:

> If you want to know whether a man lives an exemplary life, whether he's consistent, whether he can teach and model the truth, and whether he can lead people to salvation, to holiness, and to serve God, then look at the most intimate relationships in this life and see if he can do it there. Look at his family and you'll find the people who know him best, who scrutinize him most closely. Ask them about the kind of man he is.[3]

Where Leadership Starts

God posts a question in 1 Timothy 3:5—but not because he's in search of the answer. He knows it already; he just wants to make certain future pastors do as well. "For if someone does not know how to manage his own household, how will he care for God's church?" (1 Tim. 3:5).

Simply put, he can't—and shouldn't. Home is where your leadership starts.

There's a certain street-smart quality to the logic here. If it ain't working at home, why take it on the road? As the *ESV Study Bible* notes put it, "The home is the proving ground of Christian character and therefore the preparation field for ministry."[4] Or to put it another way, the home is a laboratory for the called man; it's where his skill in applying the gospel to others' lives can be measured.

The Puritans called households "little churches." The implication is clear: the quickest way to determine whether a man is qualified to lead or plant a church is to assess how effectively he's leading his chief member (his wife) and his principal congregation (his kids).

Just as the home is the hardest place to live the Christian life, it's also one of the hardest places for a pastor to apply the gospel to others' lives. Why is this? Well, for me, since the gospel is my stock-in-trade—I'm working with it all day—I'm thinking, *Do I really need to bring it home?* Also, we can offer church members gospel hope and instruction, confident that God can change hearts over time. At home, I'm not looking for gradual heart change. I'm looking for things to be different RIGHT NOW. (The gospel doesn't promise me that, although I can work up some law and guilt that insists on it.) The problem is that my family can hear me gently instruct and encourage folks in the church and wonder what kind of messes they need to create to get me to relate to them that way at home.

Brothers, let me give you a tip. If you're going to minister the gospel faithfully in the church, you've got to minister it at home. And that means it needs to penetrate your heart and life most of all. If you're able to help your wife and kids understand and appropriate the gospel, God may indeed be calling you to care for the church.

I remember being a part of an ordination service where the pastor's wife was asked to talk about her husband. She shared about the effect of her husband's gospel-inspired example upon her and the kids. She said, "He's the same at home as he appears at church; no double standards, no duplicity. If you shot footage

of our family, you'd see no surprises." The wife's words testi-
fied loudly to the man's life. They spoke volumes to the church,
both about the man's leadership, and about the God this man
was called to represent.

· · · · · · · · · · · · · · · ·

*If you're going to minister the gospel faithfully in
the church, you've got to minister it at home.*

· · · · · · · · · · · · · · · ·

When it comes to clarifying the summons, *the home offers
a primary and ongoing evidence of a pastoral calling.* For every
man who's potentially called by God to this noble office, the
church will wisely ask: How's your home?

Let's move from the general to the specific. *Dave, when
it comes to the home, what is God particularly interested in?*
Great question. Let's look together at the answer.

An Exemplary Marriage

Now don't jump off the train here. When I say exemplary, I
don't mean flawless. If a flawless marriage were the standard,
all churches would have to sack their pastors, beginning with
mine. Exemplary here means serving as an example or illustra-
tion of something.

According to the Bible, all Christian marriages are a picture
or parable pointing to the greater reality of Christ's love for the
church (Eph. 5:32). This is an astounding truth that deserves
our repeated attention, but not here and not now. Since this
isn't a marriage book, I'll limit myself to this: a believer's mar-

riage testifies to this glorious other reality. A pastor's marriage should exemplify that reality.

Kimm and I had a conflict recently. It was on a difference of opinion related to parenting one of our kids. It was a nuance thing, which is where most of parenting plays out. Anyway, she shared her opinion, and I wasn't happy. Now, since this is a guys' book and we're all part of the club, we can freely affirm something. Every husband assumes that when others don't agree with him, they just need him to talk louder and longer. So that's what I did.

I still haven't figured out what my wife doesn't get about my approach. But fortunately, God, once again, patiently showed me my anger ("How dare she question the pastor?") and stupidity (doing something that never worked before as if now it suddenly will). And Kimm, once again, was gracious to forgive. So I learned a lesson, and I think I grew a little bit. The one thing I didn't do in that situation was set an example—unless you're looking for a great example of angry stupidity. *That* was exemplary!

Look at 1 Timothy 3:2: "Therefore an overseer must be above reproach, the husband of one wife." "Above reproach" acts in an interesting way in this section of Scripture. It seems to summarize the other qualities Paul outlines. I don't think it's a stretch to see "above reproach" as an overarching value that further defines and enhances each one. This phrase calls for a pattern of life that commends, not condemns, the glorious gospel.

It's also no accident that after that phrase, the first thing listed—"the husband of one wife"—goes to the important issue of marriage. The same pattern is observed in Titus 1:6: "If anyone is above reproach, the husband of one wife." Whatever else we may infer, being above reproach is an essential qualification for pastoring, and when God moves to apply it, he looks first at marriage.

• • • • • • • • • • • • • • • •

Being above reproach is an essential qualification . . .
and when God moves to apply it,
he looks first at marriage.

• • • • • • • • • • • • • • • •

"Husband of one wife" means more than just "no concubines." Some commentators have translated the Greek phrase *mias gynaikos andra* as literally "one-woman man." I love that! If that doesn't have country song written all over it, I don't know what does. Although interpretations vary, this Greek expression seems to include at least one basic idea—the pastor is faithful to his wife. This means he doesn't have multiple wives, other sexual relationships, or anything that might bring reproach upon marriage.[5] "In this view," says Gordon Fee, "the *overseer* is required to live an exemplary married life, faithful to his *one wife* in a culture in which marital infidelity was common, and at times assumed."[6]

As you can see, the question isn't whether the pastor's marriage will exemplify something—that's a given. It's a picture of Christ and the church. The only question is, how good will the example be? God calls pastors to be models in matrimony. If you're summoned, it shows up in your marriage.

A Supportive and Accountable Wife

People love my wife. I'm serious, and I'm not just saying that because she's my wife. She has a personality that lights up a room. Invitations to travel and preach usually say, "Bring Kimm. If you can't come, send her anyway."

It's not just a personality thing. Kimm loves what God has called me to do. She loves to send me out in strength and receive me back in weakness. The way Kimm looks at it, my calling to ministry was a twofer package.

Let's face it. It's almost impossible to succeed in ministry with a wife who isn't invested. Remember, ministry isn't just a career track to something else. It's a call to see the gospel connected to people and problems. For it to work well, your wife must be convinced that you're called to ministry and she's called to follow you there.

Ministry makes a claim upon the pastor's wife. It's not something from which a husband can or should insulate her. Look at 1 Timothy 3:2: an elder must be "hospitable." It's hard to be hospitable—which basically means using your home to love and serve others—with an unsupportive wife. "My wife would love to be here tonight, but she doesn't really feel gifted for this kind of thing. And besides, it's her poker night." I don't think so.

But there's another part to this. Look at verse 11. If you agree with the ESV rendering that Paul is addressing deacons' wives (which I do), then more specifics also emerge: worthy of respect, not malicious talkers, temperate, trustworthy. What I'm saying is that if these qualities apply to wives of deacons, it's no stretch to see them applying as well to the church plant-er's wife or pastor's wife. The man may be summoned, but that summons touches both husband and wife. And it can be a little unnerving for a wife to discover that a thorough ministry assessment moves beyond her husband to her.

Now maybe you're the guy saying, "I definitely feel called, but my wife does not!" You might be surprised at how many men start there. My advice is this. Don't be anxious, but see the opportunity. Bring forth evidence of your call in the way you pastor your wife. Care for her, answer her questions, be patient, seek help from others, pray together, inspire her faith, be more patient. If the summons is there, the wife follows.

• • • • • • • • • • • • • • • •

It can be a little unnerving for a wife to discover that a thorough ministry assessment moves beyond her husband to her.

• • • • • • • • • • • • • • • •

Here's another implication you may want to consider. While both the man and his wife will need to be on the same page regarding the summons, the call is only to the man. Do you notice the pattern in Scripture? The summons is to Moses, Paul, Timothy . . . you get the picture. If we don't see this clearly, there are two ways problems can play out. One is that a wife can have her own sense of calling wrapped in an unofficial leadership role in the church. For some wives, this can stoke a wrong ambition for being seen in the church as an implied leader. Other wives can live under crushing expectations; simply because they share a bed with the pastor, they feel pressured to perform a function in the church or model something they don't have the grace to do.

And if you're single, but hear the summons, I have two words of counsel: Choose wisely! I don't think one can improve upon the way Charles Bridges punctuates this point in his classic work, *The Christian Ministry*: "How momentous therefore is the responsibility of the Minister's married choice."[7] Momentous indeed. So choose a woman who loves God, loves the gospel, and loves the church. A lady like that will follow a man like you, even to the ends of the earth.

Obedient and Faithful Children

Okay, gird up your loins, because here comes the most delicate section. This is where you're informed that if you're called to ministry, God holds you accountable for certain things about your kids that can be difficult to measure.

But let's refresh ourselves with the truth about the grace you've already received. These lists in the Pastoral Epistles are not first and foremost a standard that current pastors should be microanalyzing their lives over. If that's you, you can jump off the condemnation carousel right now. Rather, these lists are signs of the summons, evidences that God's grace is at work in a man, positioning him for church planting or pastoring. The lists are given primarily as "What to look for in selecting a pastor," and not as "Pastors must be all these things at all times or they're immediately disqualified." Paul is saying that if you're called to pastoral ministry, it will be evident to others by your leadership in the home and the behavior of your kids.

Okay, with that locked down, here's how 1 Timothy and Titus describe the called man's parenting:

- "keeping his children submissive" (1 Tim. 3:4)
- "his children are believers and not open to the charge of debauchery or insubordination" (Titus 1:6)

Now before you toss this aside in despair because you just don't know whether your kid is even converted, let me offer some pastoral tips that should shape how we read these passages. First, remember our earlier point about prior grace. If God has called you into ministry, he supplies the grace for fruitful parenting.

Second, even the best church planter or pastor in the world can't regenerate his child's heart. You can't parent a kid into conversion any more than you can pastor people into salvation. We affirm regeneration by the power of God, not by parenting. But we're called to dazzle our kids with Jesus, delight in the gospel, and train them faithfully, all while trusting the Spirit to act upon our kids. And he does!

Finally, as you can probably tell, I'm from the camp that asserts that "believers" in Titus 1:6 literally means "faithful" or submissive to parents,[8] and the next phrase concerning "debauchery or insubordination" qualifies what Paul is saying here. In other words, the kids are submissive, not indulging a lifestyle of wild living, dissipation, and rebellion against their father.[9] This passage is clearly addressing children living at home.[10]

I really like the way John Piper's congregation, Bethlehem Baptist Church, handles this issue:

It says in Titus 1:5–6 that the children of elders should be *pista* (faithful). *Tekna* is the neuter word for "children" in Greek, and *pista* agrees with it. So it is "faithful children."

Now if you just absolutize that as "they must be believers" then not only would I have had to resign, but every pastor would have to resign until his children become believers. (I'm giving you one of the arguments against it. Children become believers, they're not born believers—unless you have a very unusual view of baptism as an infant baptizer.)

So the idea would be that you can't be a pastor until they become believers—say, nobody with children under six should be a pastor. Or another take would be that if they profess faith and then walk away from it you have to leave the pastorate. . . .

So I don't think the point of those stipulations in 1 Timothy and Titus is to lead to the quick resignations of pastors, but to discern whether a man has a maturity and a giftedness to lead a well-ordered family. That's what it's for.[11]

With that in mind, here are some implications any man who has children should consider as he considers his summons.

• • • • • • • • • • • • • • • • •

Faithful parenting can generally be seen by the fruit in children's lives.

• • • • • • • • • • • • • • • • •

The simple scriptural takeaway is that faithful parenting can generally be seen by the fruit in children's lives. Kids can offer a window into the father's home management and therefore help you know whether you're being called to leadership in the church (1 Tim. 3:5). Remember, the lists aren't offered first as assessment tools to discover whether a man is disqualified, but rather what to look for in those who aspire to pastoral ministry. God invites a closer examination of children because parents are so predisposed to exaggerate how well they're doing. "Perhaps nowhere," says Charles Bridges, "are we so liable to self-deception, or so little open to conviction, as in the management of children."[12]

Seen in light of these scriptural truths, a parenting profile emerges for the man called to ministry:

- Submissive: He must lead in a manner that his children generally follow while they're being shepherded into their own faith in the Savior. They generally conform to the behavioral standards and values he sets (though these should not be viewed as something applying only to pastors' kids).
- Not open to the charge of debauchery and insubordination: He must lead in a manner that retains his influence for their moral decisions, wisely keeping before them the blessings that come from being raised in a pastor's home.
- He must lead in community: This is implied in Scripture's assumption that the church sees our kids' behavior—and, rightly or wrongly, will infer certain things from it. These passages also imply that the pastor is open to observations from others about how his family is doing.

Let's face it. A called man won't regenerate a child's heart. But he can build a home where respect, obedience, and a Godward orientation become part of the family culture. The order of that home testifies to the man's ability to celebrate and apply the gospel.

Just as the church will never be perfect and may even cause

the pastor considerable consternation at times, a pastor's home isn't immune to the workings of sin in life and relationships. But how a man handles his family trials—where he goes for help, what he trusts to make a difference, how he humbles himself, what he's willing to sacrifice for the sake of others—*that* will tell you a lot about how a man will manage a church. "The requirement concerning 'managing his own family well' is particularly important," says Vern Poythress, "because the same wisdom and skills necessary for good family management apply also to the management of God's church."[13]

Conclusion

An exemplary marriage, a supportive wife, and faithful kids unite to display a vital sign of the summons: a home that's "managed well" (1 Tim. 3:4). A man need not be perfect to have a well-managed home, but he certainly must be diligent. Part of the reason a well-managed home is such a helpful metric is that it takes most of the other qualities to produce it. It's hard to have a well-managed home when you lack self-control, or you're arrogant, or quick-tempered, or a drunkard. In those cases, the crew typically mutinies long before the ship breaks harbor for its journey.

• • • • • • • • • • • • • • • •

A called man . . . can build a home where respect, obedience, and a Godward orientation become part of the family culture.

• • • • • • • • • • • • • • • •

It's pretty amazing. God has designed Christian ministry so

that it is most effective and most God-exalting when the ministry springs from and testifies to our home lives. The family becomes a sign of the summons.

So . . . how's your family?

For Additional Study

God, Marriage, and Family, Andreas J. Köstenberger with David W. Jones
Biblical Foundations for Manhood and Womanhood, Wayne Grudem, editor
Shepherding a Child's Heart, Tedd Tripp

A Summons Story
David Martyn Lloyd-Jones: Called to Preach[1]

Sometimes the summons to preach comes with a price that might seem too high. Such was the case when David Martyn Lloyd-Jones wrestled through his call. DMLJ (as he's known by people who have to write his name a lot) was born in Cardiff, Wales, and grew up in a working class family. As a boy he had no interest in anything but sports. But somehow, at the age of thirteen, he came to the inexplicable conclusion that he was going to be a doctor. He excelled at school, and by age seventeen was beginning medical school at a prestigious London teaching hospital. He received his medical degree and was taken under wing by Lord Horder, the king's physician and the most respected medical man of his day. At an age when many young men are still trying to figure out how to balance a checkbook, DMLJ was on the fast track in a lucrative and respected professional career.

But as he launched his practice, he found himself confronted with the human condition—and the incurable illness of sin afflicting every soul. To his astonishment, he found the sharpest diagnostic light was being trained on himself. Two years into his medical career, DMLJ was brought to eternal spiritual health by the Great Physician.

The world he came into as a new Christian was not fertile ground for the gospel. Attending church was a regular part of many people's lives, but that's about it. Christianity had become a do-good religion, promoting social progress and human potential. As a young believer, DMLJ looked for spiritual mentoring, but found none in his profession. Lord Horder sought to show him all that the medical profession could offer, but ultimately it was the empty lives of the brilliant and powerful that caused

DMLJ to lose his taste for worldly success. It was then that he found a burning desire to preach Christ to the lost.

Almost immediately the young doctor began to wonder if he should leave medicine for preaching. For two years, a time of great spiritual anguish, he agonized over the decision. Although those closest to him sought to convince him that he was positioned for the most spiritual and temporal good as a Christian physician, he made a solemn declaration to follow his sense of ministry call—but then plunged into deep doubt that was eventually resolved by a renewed dedication to the medical profession.

The summons dilemma wouldn't go away, however, until he ultimately resolved to leave medicine for the pulpit. A few years later, DMLJ revealed the key to his decision, as he recalled those who questioned the rightness of it:

> I felt like saying to them, "If you knew more about the work of a doctor you would understand. We spend most of our time rendering people fit to go back to their sin!" I saw men on their sick beds, I spoke to them of their immortal souls, they promised grand things. Then they got better and back they went to their old sin! I saw I was helping these men to sin, and I decided I would do no more of it. I want to heal souls. If a man has a diseased body and his soul is all right, he is all right to the end; but a man with a healthy body and a distressed soul is all right for sixty years or so and then he has to face an eternity in hell. Ah yes! We have sometimes to give up those things which are good for that which is best of all—the joy of salvation and newness of life.[2]

Spoken with the impeccable logic of a doctor. Spoken with the impassioned burden of a preacher! DMLJ left medicine at the age of twenty-seven, and spent the next thirty years as pastor of Westminster Chapel in London. He preached for the last time in 1980, entering into glory the following year, after decades of faithfully proclaiming the gospel. His sermons and instruction for preachers are still feeding God's church today.

6

Can You Preach?

· · · · · · · · · · · · · · · · ·

As a drummer, Tommy took cool to a whole new level. Perched behind his blood-red Yamaha eight-piece double-bass drum shell pack, this dude had it going on. He presided over the equipment like a Supreme Court justice—regal, commanding, rhythmic. I sat transfixed.

Tommy was only twelve, but he was allowed to wear sweatbands on his wrist as he played, a clear symbol of adult approval, since such personal fashion statements were disallowed at our elementary school. But not for Tommy! Tommy could twirl a drumstick with one hand while riding the high hat with the other. And when he moved toward the snare, it was primal, almost violent. Tommy attacked it as if he was beating the poor drum unconscious.

As a ten-year-old just coming alive to the world of public image, I had something akin to an epiphany while watching Tommy: I was called to play drums.

As I soon discovered, there was one big problem with my dream: I had no rhythm. And I was in denial. When the band teacher was kind enough to be honest, I answered him with my knowledge of Motown and my willingness to work hard. He was patient, but he was also clear that vision was not enough. "It's about drum talent," he would say. "You haven't got any." I spent the next two years fighting for something I never possessed. What I lacked in talent, I made up for in aggressively bad drumming.

It seemed like such a fit, drums and me. I had vision and drive. The guys in the band even liked me. But the problem remained: I was rhythmically challenged. In the life of a ten-year-old, reality rarely beamed aboard for a visit. But for just a moment I listened to its sensible voice and got the message.

If a guy can't keep a beat, all the desire in the world won't make him a drummer.

If you're wondering where I'm going with this, let's invite the Prince of Preachers to make the connection. "Gentlemen," said Charles Spurgeon, "if you cannot preach, God did not call you to preach."[1] Which returns us to the question in this chapter's title.

· · · · · · · · · · · · · · · ·

If a guy can't keep a beat, all the desire in the world won't make him a drummer.

· · · · · · · · · · · · · · · ·

We're about to turn a corner here, so let's inspect the ground we've covered. For good reason, you've seen the gospel emphasized in this book. Together we've reviewed how the gospel takes death-walking, idol-worshiping, consummate fools and transforms them into children of God, disciples, and worshipers—ambassadors of the kingdom of God. We've also seen how everything we understand about the nature of the summons to ministry must be referenced from this dynamic transformation that occurs through the call of God in the gospel. This is pretty magnificent stuff.

Our conversion through the gospel is more than just a ticket to heaven; it's also a catalytic experience. Not only have we been "made . . . alive together with Christ" (Eph. 2:5), but we've also been saved "for good works, which God prepared beforehand, that we should walk in them" (2:10). Did you catch that? Because of the gospel, *there's work to do*. And that's especially and intensively true for the men God calls to church leadership. When God called Barnabas and Saul into church planting, it was no spiritual retreat. God was explicit—this was about *work*: "Set apart for me Barnabas and Saul for the work to which I have called them" (Acts 13:2).

For the next few chapters, as we continue looking at what's required in the man summoned by God, we'll move from character qualifications to the work capabilities revealed in such a man by God's grace. In this chapter, we'll examine the most glorious of these capabilities. The man divinely called is graced by God to lead through the amazing ministry of preaching.

Whatever Else You Do, Preach

If you were to write out all of the elders' requirements from the New Testament, it would represent a pretty unremarkable list. Not unimportant, and certainly not short, just unremarkable. I guess I mean that the same things expected of elders are pretty much commanded of all Christians somewhere in Scripture. And what's more, they're all about character, except for one:

the man must be "able to teach" (1 Tim. 3:2). This is the only nonnegotiable skill or talent listed in the eldership requirements. Paul unpacks it a little more for Titus: "He must hold firm to the trustworthy word as taught, so that he may be able to give instruction in sound doctrine and also to rebuke those who contradict it" (Titus 1:9).

There are a lot of things a pastor *should* be able to do. But there's clearly one thing that he *must* be able to do to hold the office. He must be able to preach.

Both these passages find a crisp summary in the last epistle Paul wrote before his death: "I charge you in the presence of God and of Christ Jesus, who is to judge the living and the dead, and by his appearing and his kingdom: preach the word; be ready in season and out of season; reprove, rebuke, and exhort, with complete patience and teaching" (2 Tim. 4:1–2).

. . . .

The Bible establishes an inseparable link between
preaching (or teaching) and pastoring.

. . . .

I don't know about you, but if Paul wanted to grab my attention for an important announcement, I don't think he could improve upon "I charge you in the presence of God and of Christ Jesus, who is to judge the living and the dead . . . *and* by his appearing . . . *and* his kingdom." With that intro, you know something pretty monumental is about to be relayed.

And what is it? Preach the Word! That's what should ultimately define ministry. There are many needs requiring a pastor's attention and voices calling for his time. But a pastor's priority is preaching. In season, out of season, it doesn't matter. Pastors must preach relentlessly, courageously, and patiently, executing their charge as those who steward the very words of God. Their congregation is the flock, and they're the shepherds. Christ's command to pastors is the same as he gave Peter: "Feed my sheep" (John 21:17).

The Bible establishes an inseparable link between preaching (or teaching) and pastoring. To be an elder, you must be able to teach; and if you're an elder, you must teach. While the New Testament cites no specific gift of "preaching," the public proclamation of God's Word is unquestionable,[2] clearly placing this noble duty to "preach the Word" at the heart of pastoral ministry. It's why Paul states it so emphatically to Timothy in the last epistle he wrote.

"The faithful preaching of the Word," writes John MacArthur, "is the most important element of pastoral ministry." He explains further:

> The God-ordained means to save, sanctify, and strengthen his church is preaching. The proclamation of the gospel is what elicits saving faith in those whom God has chosen (Romans 10:14). Through the preaching of the Word comes the knowledge of the truth that results in godliness (John 17:17; Romans 16:25; Ephesians 5:26). Preaching also encourages believers to live in the hope of eternal life, enabling them to endure suffering (Acts 14:21–22).[3]

God's people are led in a primary way through public ministry. It's that simple. Many men love God's Word, can lead effective discussions, can articulate clear doctrine, or are entertaining communicators. And these men have a significant role to play in God's church. But the grace of God to pastor is expressed through the power of preaching that imparts truth, convicts hearts, and stirs faith toward God for gospel promises. "Whatever you may know," says Charles Spurgeon, "you cannot be truly efficient ministers if you are not 'apt to teach.'"[4]

If you're called to pastor or plant a church, you're called to preach. Whether you're drawn to that or haven't given it much thought may have some bearing on whether you're hearing the summons.

Preaching Is Protection

Have you thought much about why the ability to effectively proclaim God's Word is so important for pastors? Look at it this way. If I asked you, "What was the preeminent problem for churches in the New Testament?" how would you respond? Was it lax morality? How about spiritual dullness? Too little evangelistic zeal? How about an anemic impact on the culture around them? The answer may surprise us. It's something we don't often talk about today. I'm talking about *false teachers and false doctrine*.

Do you believe it? In every New Testament letter the writer in some way goes after doctrinal problems. We're not talking about nitpicky points of theology here, but doctrinal issues that distort or undermine the glorious gospel. Why? Because getting the gospel right and keeping it right is the key to getting life right.

Pastors protect people by proclaiming and preserving the gospel. They make sure the gospel is never assumed. The stakes are too high, as D. A. Carson illustrates:

> One generation of Mennonites cherished the gospel and
> believed that the entailment of the gospel lay in certain social
> and political commitments. The next generation assumed the
> gospel and emphasized the social and political commitments.
> The present generation identifies itself with the social and
> political commitments, while the gospel is variously confessed
> or disowned; it no longer lies at the heart of the belief system
> of some who call themselves Mennonites.[5]

Gospel drift was a problem in the first-century church, and
has remained a problem throughout church history. Because of
that continuing threat, the elder has to "hold firm to the trustworthy word as taught, so that he may be able to *give instruction in sound doctrine* and also to *rebuke those who contradict
it*" (Titus 1:9). Paul underlined this requirement through his
personal exhortation to Titus: "As for you, *teach what accords
with sound doctrine*" (Titus 2:1). Sound doctrine distinguishes
truth from error; it sets the preacher in truth, and truth in the
preacher.

Preaching sound doctrine means you're keeping the gospel
crystal clear and at the center of everything you teach and do.
The man called by God can grasp in increasing measure how
the gospel links to life. He connects adversity, suffering, marriage, money, kids, death—the stuff of life—all to the gospel. As
he does this, the gospel is built into the church and the church is
built upon the gospel.

Sadly, our cultural view of preaching is largely formed by
what we see on TV. Now, the men (or women) I've seen on the
tube are invariably gifted speakers. Some of them can *preach*—I
mean it's hard to take my eyes off them. But if you look past the

delivery, the cadence, the carefully crafted words, and the volume, it doesn't take long to realize that a magnetic TV presence doesn't cut it. A preacher needs more than delivery. He needs content. He needs the gospel.

. . . .

Gospel drift . . . has remained a problem throughout church history.

. . . .

And brothers, don't think that simply being able to present sound doctrine, argue it from the pulpit, and illustrate it from real life is the point. The gospel isn't content alone. It's content that reveals Jesus Christ. If we can preach gospel truths in a way that leaves people indifferent to the Savior who fills the gospel with meaning, we're not preaching the gospel. We don't proclaim a truth matrix. We carry the "great and excellent thing," Calvin says, for which leaders are "set over the Church, that they may represent the person of the Son of God."[6]

How Preachers Are Made

Ever had a GPS with a poor sense of direction? Mine's like that. Or it hates me. Or it's possessed.

Recently I was speaking at an evening meeting. I carefully loaded the exact address into my GPS and followed the calm voice guiding me through a maze of streets in this unfamiliar city. The final command delivered me to an empty lot in the wrong part of town staring at a stripped car on cinder blocks. When I called a guy at the meeting location, he informed me

I was twenty-five minutes away. That's when I heard the GPS snicker at me.

So I punched it. Why not? There are few things more useless than a directionally challenged GPS.

Fortunately, as we're discovering, the summons to church plant or pastor offers a clearer course. The summons to pastor is a call to preach. If that's you, get ready for God to fashion you into a preacher. That process will be exhilarating, but it won't be effortless. Bishop William A. Quayle, in 1910, was asked if preaching is "the art of making a sermon and delivering it." And he answered, "Why, no, that is not preaching. Preaching is the art of making a preacher and delivering that."[7]

If God is creating that in you, get ready for a ride. Certain desires will stir in your heart, and circumstances will arise that you never planned. Here are a few things God will do in you and require of you if he is making you into a preacher.

Study Diligently

"Do your best to present yourself to God as one approved, a worker who has no need to be ashamed, rightly handling the word of truth" (2 Tim. 2:15).

Paul tells Timothy to *do his best* in handling the Word of God. To handle it right, we need to study it well. The summons puts study at the top of the "to do" list of the pastor.

I believe one reason Paul makes this a priority is that study is never a squeaky wheel. It doesn't text you and ask to meet for coffee. Study doesn't spam your inbox with offers you can't resist, or ping you on a daily basis. If you don't seek study, it won't seek you. And the only way to consistently seek study is to learn to love it—to want it when everything else in ministry wants you.

To cultivate an enduring desire to study, we need to build a library. Think of a theological library as a "college of teachers" who are committed to helping you do your best to handle the Word of truth. Choose your library carefully, leaning heaviest on those who have stood the test of time. Consult it regularly, not just collecting books, but reading them. Any pastor who thinks he has all he needs to handle the Bible will find himself eventually in that "ashamed" category that Paul warns Timothy about. That's why I've always told aspiring pastors that *you must read to lead.*

Reading feeds. It opens our souls to a long line of counselors. Discontent? Sit with Thomas Watson and invite his diagnosis. Empty? Read Edwards and be filled. Maligned? Read Spurgeon's biography and gain perspective. Perplexed? Let B. B. Warfield unravel complicated things with piercing theological and biblical clarity.

And not just the dead guys. I mean, think about it—there are authors alive now who'll still be read a century from now. But we don't need to wait a hundred years. Reading them now will feed us so that we in turn can nourish others.

One of Paul's last directives to Timothy was this: "When you come, bring . . . the books, and above all the parchments" (2 Tim. 4:13). When study stuff makes it into a man's final words, you know study has become pretty important. If you've heard the summons, it will be important to you as well.

Be Ready to Suffer

Luther said three things make the theologian: *oratio* (prayer), *meditatio* (meditation), and *tentatio* (tribulation).[8] I think the same might be said of preachers. Paul's description of ministry would never make it into a seminary advertisement: "We are afflicted in every way, but not crushed; perplexed, but not driven to despair; persecuted, but not forsaken; struck down, but not destroyed" (2 Cor. 4:8–9). But it's the conclusion he draws that I find most striking: "So death is at work in us, but life in you" (2 Cor. 4:12).

It's pretty amazing, but Paul seemed to conclude that there was some benefit transmitted to the Corinthians because he suffered. Suffering positioned him spiritually to be a better leader, a more comforting voice. "If we are afflicted," Paul said, "it is for your comfort and salvation; and if we are comforted, it is for your comfort" (2 Cor. 1:6). That's a ton of comfort he's talking about there. More importantly, he's talking about a leadership principle that comes with the call. It's Romans 8:28 for leaders: *God causes the pastor's suffering to work together for the people's good.*

John Piper is way more eloquent on this point than I could ever be, so listen in on how he says it:

> God never wastes the gift of suffering (Philippians 1:29). It is given to His ministers as He knows best, and its design is the consolation and salvation of our people. No pastoral suffering is senseless. No pastoral pain is pointless. No adversity is absurd and meaningless. Every heartache has its divine target in the consolation of the saints, even when we feel least useful.[9]

Here's the take away: comfort comes through the preaching

of an afflicted man. So God will ordain trials to help you pastor and preach. Hardly a strong sales pitch for ministry, I know. After all, where in the engineer's job description does it say, "Job Objective: to suffer in order to enhance engineering skills"? But that's the way God arranged things for pastors.

Still want to be in ministry?

Be Vigilant

"Keep a close watch on yourself and on the teaching. Persist in this, for by so doing you will save both yourself and your hearers" (1 Tim. 4:16). Watch yourself. Watch your teaching. Persist in this so you and your people are saved.

Wow. That certainly raises the stakes. Somehow, there's a link between the church's perseverance and my persistent self-examination. In fact, my self-examination needs to cover not only my life but also my teaching. Let me say it again—*wow!*

The call to ministry is a call to watching. We evaluate ourselves, we evaluate our teaching, we invite evaluation from others, and we enjoy the scrutiny of the church. If, as Socrates said, "the unexamined life is not worth living," then ministry must be the high life.

Here's my suggestion. If you're wrestling over your call, start asking yourself some heart-scanning questions. Invite others into your life and ask them to watch as well. Ask your pastor for opportunities to share the Word and then solicit evaluation. Find a way for others to help you "watch your teaching."

For example, when I served in Sovereign Grace Churches, we developed a tool called the e-5 to help measure the capabilities of a man who wants to plant a church. The "e" means essential, so these are the essential five qualities. Guess what the first and most important factor is? You guessed it—preaching! But the tool gets really specific on some different aspects of preaching that help us measure it through the experience of the listener. Take a look.

- The *gospel* factor: Does the man's preaching move people toward the gospel?
- The *Bible* factor: Does he have an aptitude for doctrine? Does he exegete Scripture competently?
- The *eagerness* factor: Do people get excited when they hear he's scheduled to preach?
- The *people* factor: Does he communicate in a way that helps people? Do people say they feel like he understands them and relates the Bible to the issues they're facing?
- The *cohesive* factor: Are his messages clear and easy to follow?
- The *guest* factor: Are visitors inclined to come back and hear him preach again? Do his sermons make the gospel clear to unbelievers?

There are others as well, but you get the gist.

If you don't have many opportunities to preach, maybe explore how this type of tool might apply to the way you lead a Bible study or prayer meeting. Do you lead worship? How do your comments between songs preach? You can even think through this if you do a lot of personal ministry or counseling.

God's People Need Preachers

Today's fields cry out for men who can organize thoughts and communicate doctrine in ways that display God's glory and incite corresponding affections. God is calling for men who can speak his words after him—men who use language skillfully, like a doctor wisely choosing the best treatment after studying the affliction. Be it in preaching or teaching or counseling, these men will make God's Word plain, understandable, compelling, and applicable. They are, after all, God's ambassadors, and ambassadors are duty-bound to make their sender's message clear and effective.

• • • • • • • • • • • • • • • •

If you're wrestling over your call, start asking yourself some heart-scanning questions.

• • • • • • • • • • • • • • • •

The preacher of God's Word will draw people and lift their vision to God. "To be able to gather a congregation," says Charles Chaney, "is the seal of one's call."[10] And what causes a congregation to gather around such a called leader is effective preaching. This phenomenon—the gathering and returning of people to hear our exposition—is a biblical and time-tested validation of our calling. And it's why the church, by God's grace, will appropriately ask a straightforward question about you or any man potentially called by God to ministry: *Can he preach?*

For Additional Study
Christ-Centered Preaching, Bryan Chapell
The Supremacy of God in Preaching, John Piper
Between Two Worlds, John R. W. Stott
Preaching and Preachers, D. Martyn Lloyd-Jones

A Summons Story
James Montgomery Boice: A Shepherd in the City[1]

James Montgomery Boice was a shepherd called to the city. Born in Pittsburgh in 1938, Boice was thirty when he came to his first pastorate at Tenth Presbyterian Church in Philadelphia. Though a scholar by training, he wanted to invest his life in pastoral ministry. He viewed his calling to Tenth Presbyterian not as a launching pad for other ministry, but as a commitment to the people he was called to serve.

To shepherd in the city required a man willing to build a church for the future without forsaking its past. He understood his place in a tradition of great preaching and great leadership at Tenth Presbyterian. Yet he came to the church when Philadelphia was in economic and social decay. Longtime members were leaving the city for safer suburban churches. Under Boice, the church built a spiritual firewall. It created ministries to reach the diverse urban population. Tenth Presbyterian became a place where the poor received mercy, students found fellowship, business people found vision, the sexually troubled found refuge, and the lost heard the gospel. Under Boice's leadership, sheep were added and found care. Boice once said, "For 150 years this church has taught the Word of God. . . . That work is not yet done. It has to be done age after age."[2]

To shepherd in the city required a man committed to truth and the defense of it. Boice not only protected the wall of the church, but he also turned the church into a fortress of sound doctrine and biblical fidelity. When the church's denomination drifted away from historic Christian faith, Boice led the church to a new, productive affiliation. He became an internationally known spokesman for clear and thoughtful declaration of truth in the postmodern world, writing gospel-centered commentaries and pastoral theology and becoming one of the founders of the Alliance for Confessing Evangelicals. Boice knew pastoral ministry was more than believing truth; it was defending the truth you believe. Or as he put it, "The issue is not just where we stand, but why we stand where we do."

Finally, to shepherd in the city required a man who would live out his doctrine before the people he was called to serve. In the spring of 2000, Boice found out he had cancer with only a few weeks to live. Loving his people to the very end, he stood one Sunday and shared what God was showing him in the face of death:

> If I were to reflect on what goes on theologically here, there are two things I would stress. One is the sovereignty of God. That's not novel. We have talked about the sovereignty of God here forever. God is in charge. When things like this come into our lives, they are not accidental. It's not as if God somehow forgot what was going on, and something bad slipped by. . . . God does everything according to his will. We've always said that.
>
> But what I've been impressed with mostly is something in addition to that. It's possible, isn't it, to conceive of God as sovereign and yet indifferent? God's in charge, but he doesn't care. But it's not that. God is not only the one who's in charge; God is also good. Everything he does is good. And what Romans 12, verses 1 and 2, says is that we have the opportunity by the renewal of our minds—that is, how we think about these things—actually to prove what God's will is. And then it says, "His good, pleasing, and perfect will." Is that good, pleasing, and perfect to God? Yes, of course, but the point of it is that it's good, pleasing, and perfect to us. If God does something in your life, would you change it? If you'd change it, you'd make it worse. It wouldn't be as good.

So that's the way we want to accept it and move forward—and who knows what God will do?[3]

To be a shepherd, you must commit yourself to the sheep. Your doctrine will be their doctrine when you live it out before them. And with that, who knows what God will do?

7

Can You Shepherd?

. . . .

The fisherman now a shepherd. From a social and economic standpoint, Peter's stock was tanking. But that hardly mattered. The call was clear, personal, unmistakable, issued by the Savior himself. Peter would never forget . . . *could* never forget.

The events of that single week were nothing short of cataclysmic. Some of the memories were so excruciating, only God could redeem them. Jesus, the one to whom Peter confessed, "You are the Christ, the Son of the living God" (Matt. 16:16), was crucified right before their very eyes. He died naked and nailed to a cross—tortured, bloodied, abandoned, alone, friendless.

Peter was devastated. It was a nightmare come to life. God came, God loved, God died. What happens now? There was no going back and no moving forward. Peter was stuck in a gloomy twilight, caught between shame and despair. Those few days were like a storm-tossed ship fighting to stay afloat against gales of guilt. The nights—well, he couldn't even speak of them. They were too dark for words.

Peter, the rock, the one who boldly announced his loyalty and fidelity, "Lord, I am ready to go with you both to prison and to death" (Luke 22:33), had failed—miserably. No matter how he tried to justify it, the raw truth was inescapable. He had lied to save his skin—three times.

But then it happened: news of a sighting. The crucified Jesus had risen from death. He had come to them all—speaking peace. But he hadn't spoken to Peter. What would the Savior say to his most foolish disciple?

The answer came one morning. Peter found Jesus cooking breakfast. The Creator of all things was frying fish. They ate without speaking. Maybe there was hope for a coward after all.

Then Jesus broke the silence, saying, "Simon, son of John, do you love me more than these? . . . Feed my lambs." Again: "Tend my sheep." And again: "Feed my sheep" (John 21: 15–17). It was unmistakable. Peter was forgiven. Peter was summoned. The fisherman was to become a shepherd.

The Fellow Elder and You

One must wonder whether that memory was washing over Peter, thirty years later. With the clouds of persecution gathering under the storm of Nero's insanity, the dispersed Christians in Asia needed hope. They would suffer. They needed shepherds. Compelled by the Spirit, Peter wrote to them:

> So I exhort the elders among you, as a fellow elder and a witness of the sufferings of Christ, as well as a partaker in the glory that is going to be revealed: shepherd the flock of God that is among you, exercising oversight, not under compulsion, but willingly, as God would have you; not for shameful gain, but eagerly; not domineering over those in your charge, but being

examples to the flock. And when the chief Shepherd appears, you will receive the unfading crown of glory. (1 Pet. 5:1–4)

If we've learned anything so far, it's this: the summons isn't first about what we must do, but about what God has done in Christ and what God provides for those called to lead his church.

With that established, we need to perform a prelanding checkup of what we're summoned to do. So trays up and seats forward as we touch down on a question that will largely reveal whether you understand the point of this whole journey: *Can you shepherd?* To explore what that really means, let's return to Peter.

How Do I Know If I Can Shepherd?

For some people the word "shepherd" brings to mind watercolor paintings in church nurseries. The shepherd is cradling a lamb while the sun sets behind him in splashes of splendor. Or he's leaning on his shepherd staff looking out over a Crayola-green field. He's got blue eyes and long wavy hair, his gaze is solemn, his robe spotless.

But when Peter said "shepherd," his readers back then would picture a ruddy livestock worker. This guy is on the clock 24/7, scouting out pastures, corralling strays, dispensing first aid, fixing broken bones, making sure the sheep are safe and well fed. This dude works hard, gets dirty, and even knows how to go ninja with his staff.

When Peter tells elders to "shepherd the flock of God," he has all this in mind. A shepherd of God's people is responsible to care for them. He's responsible to feed them the Word of God in his preaching, counseling, even everyday conversations. He's responsible to protect the sheep from false teachers, from the poison of false doctrine, from the influence of the world. There's a reason that "shepherd" is the most prominent metaphor in Scripture for a pastor's role. "The fundamental responsibility of church leaders," says Tim Witmer, "is to shepherd God's flock."[1] Your success in ministry is always linked with their welfare. Doing that well starts with knowing what it means.

Over the next several pages we'll look at how Peter describes "shepherding the flock of God." We'll jump around in 1 Peter 5 a little, but I think you'll see that everything we talk about is rooted in the text.

Will You Care?

"Shepherd the flock of God that is among you" (1 Pet. 5:2). It's a strange imperative, this command to elders—makes one feel that God takes it pretty seriously. "Shepherd the flock of God that is among you." No called man can just breeze by it. It tells him something significant, something urgent. If you think you're called, listen up.

What does it mean to care for the flock of God? *It means willing and eager oversight.* In previous chapters we've discussed being examples to the flock, so let's move to the other portions of this text. "Exercising oversight" is actually only one Greek word: *episkopeo*. It literally means "to look upon" and includes the idea of looking carefully or watching diligently. In his book *Shepherds After My Own Heart*, Timothy Laniak defines it as "a vigilant attention to threats that can disperse or destroy the flock."[2] The shepherd is a guardian with boots on the ground, ready to be used by the Chief Shepherd to guide and protect his flock.

. . . .

The shepherd . . . has the limitless resources of God to do what a shepherd needs to do in any circumstance.

. . . .

Imagine your country was invaded by an army hostile to Christianity. Now imagine you're the pastor of the church facing persecution (it's happening to some servant of God even as you read this). To truly honor the Chief Shepherd and serve his flock, you would need to be more than gifted and available. You would need to be "willing, as God would have you" (1 Pet. 5:2). The shepherd doesn't run when the heat comes. He has nowhere to go in an earthly sense, but he has the limitless resources of God to do what a shepherd needs to do in any circumstance—because "God would have him" do it.

It means love. Practically speaking, shepherding means loving people. You can't love ministry and be annoyed by people. The summons is a call to love sheep.

"To love to preach," Lloyd-Jones says, "is one thing; to love those to whom we preach is quite another."[3] A man summoned by God to lead his flock loves both. And both are essential to the task. The study and reflection required of a pastor isn't meant to turn him into an academic hermit; instead his study must lead him to more effectively nurture the church. He must possess a basic capacity to communicate God's heart and God's love to God's people.

And this love must be sturdy. *USA Today* did a front-page story two days before Christmas on today's shepherd. The article described how hundreds of Peruvian shepherds are brought to America each year. These are some seriously rough dudes. They know how to fight off a mountain lion to rescue a sheep, and they castrate a lamb the old-fashioned way—with their teeth. Fortunately, pastors are spared such delicate tasks, but the love they display often demands a similar toughness.

When a sheep strays, a good shepherd will go after them with a love that speaks truth. Sometimes, brothers, a pastor has to sacrifice being liked in order to express love. People ensnared in sin want "support" and "understanding," which in our world usually means freedom to do what they want regardless of the commands of God's Word. To love people means we care enough to be part of God's disciplining process—always merciful and humble, but resolutely committed to God's glory as well. Sometimes it takes a tough love from a gentle shepherd to save a soul from death. The summons to shepherd is a call to a sturdy biblical love.

It means connecting care to the Chief Shepherd. The local church immerses shepherds in the stuff of life. Consider the mysteries of human experience—the childless couple who just had their third miscarriage, the new believer still entangled in lifelong addiction, the hardworking provider who just lost a job, the dying sinner confronting the certainty of judgment. This is no TV drama. It's reality!

In those despairing moments, who is appointed to guide

God's people through the inexplicable valleys to drink in the streams of God's providence and goodness? Who will remind us that the Chief Shepherd is a Good Shepherd (John 10:11)? None other than the shepherds of the church. What a glorious display of God's grace to create a special office for our care during times of trial and suffering. Far from the spotlights of conferences and media Christianity, caring shepherds labor in obscurity to tend people's souls. They connect sheep to the Chief Shepherd.

For me this has made a huge difference over the last three decades as trials and difficulties have pressed in. Raising teens, physical ailments, marriage disagreements, ministry setbacks— and that's all just last month! If not for the skill of loving shepherds who directed me to the Chief Shepherd and the soul-satisfying truth of his gospel, I'd be making dust cloths in a padded cell under the careful watch of my new friends in white jackets. But thanks to my pastors' care, I now love God more deeply and apply the gospel more thoroughly.

Will You Lead?

Make no mistake. Shepherding is leadership and leadership is shepherding.[4] It's impossible to "exercise oversight" (1 Pet. 5:2) and not lead. But leadership is often like an empty glass—you can fill it with any definition you want. What does it mean for a shepherd to be gifted to lead? How do you know if you have that gift?

Let's first remember that leadership begins with grace. God's treasury of grace is discovered in the most extraordinary places, and one of them is in the gift of leadership. God gives certain men grace in the form of an ability to lead the church.

Paul instructs us in Romans 12, "Having gifts that differ *according to the grace given to us*, let us use them." Then he lists various gifts and tells us how to use them well. Included there is this statement: "the one who leads, with zeal" (Rom. 12:6–8). The gift is leadership; the encouragement is to use this gift "with zeal" (or "with diligence," as several versions say). Though God has spread his gifts to everyone in the church, he has given certain men a gift of leadership. These men should be identified, then encouraged to lead zealously.

What does this gift of leadership look like in pastoral ministry? Let me offer you some "leadership factors" I've observed in men who wear the mantle of shepherd well. Don't grade yourself—gifts emerge over time, often in preparation for specific tasks. But this could help you get a better handle on your strengths and weaknesses as they might play out in pastoral leadership.

- The "preaching-as-leading" factor: You can establish a preaching diet for the church that sets direction and feeds souls.
- The "follow him" factor: People talk about the impact you have on their lives. Other gifted people want to glean from your life.
- The "make it happen" factor: When you see a need or a problem, you think solutions and action.
- The "can you see it" factor: You can see the big picture and have confidence for the future. And when you talk to other people, they see it too.

- The "order from chaos" factor: You understand the value of planning, organization, and efficiency. Your life doesn't look like an unmade bed.
- The "mobilize the troops" factor: You know the best way to have impact is not to do it all yourself. You love to put people in places where they can be effective and fruitful.
- The "learn to lead" factor: You're not content with what you know. You study in order to grow in understanding.
- The "godly ambition" factor: You're not interested in settling in or shrinking back from challenges. You want to do all you can for the advance of the kingdom of God.

Once I was involved in bringing closure to an urban church about five years after it started. The church enjoyed meaningful relationships and passionate teaching, but it began to stagnate. Crucial signs of viability weren't there. No one was ignorant of the need for urban churches and the challenges of planting them, and to make the decision to fold it back into the sending church was heart-wrenching for everyone—including me. But through it all we saw wonderfully the presence of the Lord through the humility of the church planter himself. As he looked back on the plant, he recognized he didn't possess sufficient leadership as a church planter to truly shepherd the church.

This heroic church planter was astute enough to realize that leadership limitations can create church limitations. Rather than selfishly grasping the helm, he humbly considered whether his lack of leadership gifting might be God redirecting him away from church planting. He was asking the right questions. Years later he's in full-time pastoral ministry, serving on a team where his gifts can flourish and his weaknesses are covered by the others' strengths.

Will You See Your Need for a Team?

"I exhort the elders among you, as a fellow elder . . . being examples to the flock" (1 Pet. 5:1, 3). Ministry was a lonely place for Ted. The church plant was up and running. The vision that had fueled his prayers for years was now happening all around him. He was a busy man and everybody needed him. But Ted was experiencing something he never expected. He was lonely. It was a strange kind of loneliness. His marriage was doing well; he loved spending time with his family. But when he stepped into his office, it was like walking into an isolation chamber. He talked to people all day long, helping them, directing them, encouraging them—and he certainly heard their appreciation. But there were burdens he had to carry, confidences he had to keep, fears he had to battle—things nobody else could really understand; not his wife, nor his friends, nor his ministry leaders. Ted loved being a pastor. But if he were honest, it was wearisome. He never thought ministry would feel so . . . *remote*.

Sadly, there are a lot of Teds who get swallowed up in the loneliness of pastoral ministry. Some men soldier through heroically, finding God's grace through years of isolation. But tragically, far too many gifted and sincere guys wash out in ministry due, in some way, to the isolation. Some tumble down the steps of immorality or experience the devastation of a shattered marriage—studies show that 75 percent of men who fall into sexual misconduct "indicated that they were lonely and isolated."[5] But a lot of guys just quietly close it down, get the insurance license, and move on with life.

Maybe you're thinking, "Okay, Dave, I get the point. I'm going to make sure I work in a church with a pastoral staff.

Then I won't be lonely." Maybe . . . but maybe not. It appears another big reason guys leave ministry is they get tired of the competition with other leaders in the church.[6] So here you are, ready to take the plunge into pastoral ministry, and I've just ruled out both doing it by yourself and doing it on a staff. What's the other option—cloning?

. . . .

*Church leadership in the New Testament was a
shared endeavor. . . . It's known as team ministry.*

. . . .

I think Peter gives us the answer if we're willing to see it. In a word, it's *plurality*. If you're not familiar with that word, hang in there. Plurality is just a way to describe the scriptural evidence that church leadership in the New Testament was a shared endeavor.[7] In the lingo of the twenty-first century, it's known as team ministry.

Where do we see that in 1 Peter 5? If you look at the plain reading, you can't comprehend Peter's foundational instruction for pastors without seeing the plurality. He addresses elder*s*, with an "s." In fact, elders in the New Testament are always plural,[8] apart from Peter's self-reference here as he addresses them as a "fellow elder" (5:1). Peter's ministry is joined with others, who are to be "examples" (5:3) to the flock. In the New Testament, churches ideally had more than one leader.

In fact, I'm not sure you can responsibly apply Peter's instructions as a shepherd, or any other New Testament text about shepherding ministry, as if pastoring is a one-man show. As one commentator puts it, "The apostolic churches seem, in general, to have had a plurality of elders."[9] In *Biblical Eldership*, Alexander Strauch states that "on the local church level, the New Testament plainly witnesses to a consistent pattern of shared pastoral leadership."[10]

Now, I understand there may be seasons where a man is laboring alone in local church ministry. Some church planters certainly experience this. If that's you, my heart goes out to you and my respect for you sails off the charts. And I'm not going to tell you there's a certain way a church has to be governed to make team ministry possible. I've seen team ministry done in churches with different polity structures. It's not about the structures. It's about humbly recognizing that men need community to lead well, and the church needs a community of leaders. As a friend once told me, "A team's wisdom is better than one man's genius."

If I were writing a book on church polity (how churches are governed), I'd launch into a detailed study of the biblical witness for plurality of leadership. But then you may fall asleep. So if you're looking for a little narcolepsy remedy, here are some quick things to ponder. Team ministry done well provides:

- a place for men with diverse gifts to contribute their individual strengths to church government
- relational support for pastors amid the inevitable trials and temptations of ministry
- a multitude of counsel in major decisions
- protection against the domination of one or two strong personalities

- flexibility to arrange staffing to fit the changing needs of the church
- multigenerational perspective for the church as young men and seasoned veterans all sit at the same table of responsibility

Brothers, you don't want to do ministry without other men or in competition with other men. It's a recipe for burnout or blowup. Ministry is hard enough as it is. Why take on a burden that God doesn't intend you to have?

If you think you're receiving a summons from the Great Shepherd to shepherd his people, you need to be thinking hard *right now* about the biblical necessity of team ministry. Put your life in community now so that team will come easier then. Don't make choices that deliver you into Ted's seclusion. Lonely and isolated is for prisoners, not for pastors.

Will You Keep Christ First?

As Peter "a witness of the sufferings of Christ, as well as a partaker in the glory that is going to be revealed," exhorts these elders to "shepherd the flock of God," he has many things on his mind (1 Pet. 5:1). He must cover issues of care and authority. He must give clarity on proper motivations for ministry. He must offer help for believers suffering and about to suffer. Peter knows the terrain well. But we can't approach this passage—and we can't understand what it means to be a shepherd—without taking note of where he starts and ends. We've touched on this already, but it's worth whatever refocus you can give it. If you take away one thing here, make it this: to Peter, shepherding was about Christ.

"A witness of the sufferings of Christ, as well as a partaker in the glory that is going to be revealed." Sure, Peter was referencing his unique authority to speak to elders. The raising of Lazarus, the night at Gethsemane, Christ's arrest and crucifixion—Peter had seen it all! As a principal player among the original Twelve, he had a unique role as a companion of Christ and an eyewitness to his suffering.

But it's more than that. Peter saw Christ as glorious. Christ's sufferings, his return, his rewards—all this pointed to a magnificent Savior crucified and raised in glory. Jesus is the Chief Shepherd who cares for all the sheep. He's the Chief, and all shepherding is done under him and because of him.

. . . .

People will suffer, and they'll need to hear the voice of earthly shepherds reminding them of the Chief Shepherd's care.

. . . .

Gentlemen, Peter is modeling something for every generation of pastors. People will suffer, and they'll need to hear the voice of earthly shepherds reminding them of the Chief Shepherd's care. If you're called to ministry, you must remember that Christ is the Chief Shepherd, not you. Our role is to bear witness to him. As Edmund Clowney said, "Peter would prepare his fellow elders to bear their witness by mirroring the gospel in their lives."[12]

When you step into pastoral ministry, you're going to want to help people. And you'll probably have a lot of great thoughts on what people need. But trust me on this: you don't have what they really need. What you do have is Christ. Keep his suffering and his glory first. The married couple in conflict needs that from you. So does the struggling single mom with two teens. And the father who was just diagnosed with cancer. So follow Peter's example. When you exhort people who are suffering or serving, remind them of the Savior. Bear witness to his suffering for them, speak splendidly about his return to get them, counsel boldly about his power to change them.

Always a Shepherd, Never Alone

Once I was at a church-planting conference where a ministry veteran made the following observations. About four thousand churches are started each year in the United States. That's encouraging. But then he noted that seven thousand close their doors every year. Some fifteen hundred pastors leave ministry every month—a total of eighteen thousand a year. Only 10 percent of pastors remain in ministry until age sixty-five.[13]

At another such conference, one man described his recent church-planting experience in a midsize American city. During his first year of church planting, twenty-five other churches were being planted in that same area. Twenty-five! But it was the man's next words that sent chills through the room. After only a few years, his church was the only one still in operation.

I hear that and think, *What happened to all those pastors?* Seriously, what happens to these men who apparently burned with a desire for ministry? Maybe, like Ted, they found themselves alone and lost the zeal. Maybe the problems of the sheep were bigger than their faith to deal with them. Maybe opposition drove them from the task. Maybe they realized their gifts weren't the right mix for the job they were given. Hopefully, they're bearing fruit in ministry that fits them.

In any case it saddens my heart when men lose churches and churches lose men. Because Peter reminds us that one day the Chief Shepherd will appear, and will give crowns of glory (1 Pet. 5:4) to his faithful servants. Nothing is more important for keeping men in ministry than the reminder that the Savior will come again! Until then, men must stand tall and be prepared to answer this question: *Can you shepherd?*

For Additional Study

Shepherds After My Own Heart, Timothy Laniak

The Shepherd Leader, Timothy Z. Witmer

Instruments in the Redeemer's Hands, Paul David Tripp

The Reformed Pastor, Richard Baxter

A Summons Story
Charles Spurgeon: Loving the Lost[1]

You can tell a lot about a man by what makes him happy. And you can tell what makes a minister happy by what he gives himself to most deeply. When it comes to Charles Spurgeon, it's pretty obvious what made him happy—the ministry of preaching. After all, the man's printed sermons total over twenty million words! He's estimated to have preached to ten million people in his lifetime—including over twenty-three thousand in one meeting. He's the most widely published Christian author in history, and nearly everything of his in print is a sermon. No wonder he's called "the Prince of Preachers."

But Spurgeon wasn't driven only by a desire to preach. What drove him into the pulpit, into meetings with countless people, and into training ministers through his Pastor's College, planting churches, and fueling missions, was one consuming desire: Spurgeon loved the lost!

Consider the evidence. One biographer summed up Spurgeon's ministry this way:

> Spurgeon's preaching has been evaluated, his writings analyzed, his philanthropy considered, and his political involvement summarized. However it was the role of Pastor/Evangelist which dominated his ministry. Evangelism was at the heart of all he sought to do. Whether preaching from the pulpit or speaking with individuals, Spurgeon was always an evangelist. The many avenues of evangelical ministry all arose from his consuming passion for souls.[2]

A Baptist historian concurs, quoting Spurgeon himself:

> From all our congregations a bitter cry should go up unto God, unless conversions are continually seen. If our preaching never

saves a soul, and is not likely to do so, should we not better glorify God as peasants, or as tradesmen? What honour can the Lord receive from useless ministers? The Holy Ghost is not with us, we are not used of God for his gracious purposes, unless souls are quickened into heavenly life. Brethren, can we bear to be useless? Can we be barren, and yet content?[3]

The cynic might say, "Yeah, if I had Spurgeon's gifting, I could preach and easily expect the conversions to come." But Spurgeon made a distinction between the gift to preach and the heart for the lost. One was a gift to be deployed in service, the other a motivation for service. As he once said, "I would rather be the means of saving a soul from death than be the greatest orator on earth."[4] God's call to Spurgeon, as it is to any preacher, was to seek the lost souls around him; preaching just happened to be the means of grace at his disposal.

Brothers, if you aspire to emulate the Prince of Preachers, don't look first to the man's pulpit or his programs. Look to his passion. Here's Spurgeon's:

If sinners will be damned, at least let them leap to hell over our bodies. And if they will perish, let them perish with our arms about their knees, imploring them to stay. If hell must be filled, at least let it be filled in the teeth of our exertions, and let not one go there unwarned and unprayed for.[5]

8

Do You Love the Lost?

. . . .

"We don't care," they said. "Cough up the cash."

I was shocked.

I mean, that wasn't exactly what they said, but it sure felt that way. The bank letter said payment on my school loan must begin immediately. But I was unemployed and almost penniless—there was no money. I wrote an appeal to their compassion. They countered with a clause from my contract. Hard times or not, it was my responsibility to start cutting checks. I may have been confused, but the contract was clear. Another education had just begun. Know the terms before you sign. Check!

Were you surprised when you read the chapter title? Maybe you're thinking, "Yo, Dave, I thought this was about pastoral ministry. What's up with the evangelism thing? Let's get back to pastor stuff and tell me how I can preach like Spurgeon." If all you want to do is preach like Spurgeon, that's easy. Just take a genius brain that makes theology simple and attach it to an almost supernatural command of language. So . . . forget about preaching like Spurgeon. And he'd rather you think about evangelism anyway.

A lot of guys thinking about calling are thinking *pastor* because they're thinking, *O Lord, not evangelism!* But the church is made up of the evangelized, and those people have to come from somewhere. The gospel is for everyone, which means the summons to be a pastor doesn't stop with the saved. So if you're called to preach the gospel, you're called to interact with the people who don't have it. That's the deal. And like my loan, these terms are nonnegotiable. A call to ministry is a call to labor among the lost.

• • • • • • • • • • • • • • • •

A call to ministry escorts the man beyond the comfortable confines of the church community.

• • • • • • • • • • • • • • • •

In the last chapter of his final epistle, Paul urges Timothy, "Do the work of an evangelist" (2 Tim. 4:5). Paul is conveying the terms of effective pastoral ministry for Timothy and all who follow. Tucked between the calls to preach, to be sound in doctrine, and to fulfill his ministry lies this unavoidable command. A call to ministry escorts the man beyond the comfortable confines of the church community. It's a call to gospel work in the world.

Pastor Mark Dever, who models this pastor/evangelist burden as well as any pastor alive, lays it out clearly:

> I generally know, when someone goes into the ministry because they like to work only with Christians and to do church things, that this person probably isn't called. The person who is usually best is the person who is quite good in a non-Christian work environment but who is willing, for the sake of the king-

dom, to be called back "behind the lines" as it were, to spend his life supplying those who are on the front lines of ministry. As a pastor, I am in a position that is both frustrating and privileged. It is frustrating in that I really enjoy opportunities to spend time with non-Christian friends, relatives, and neighbors. Because I am a pastor, I have to work intentionally to create such opportunities. But my position is also a privileged one, in that I get to meet at least weekly with a few hundred people and work to equip them to share the Gospel with their friends and family during the week ahead. Being a minister of the Word is a calling that has its price in personal evangelistic opportunities but that also affords great opportunities to encourage others.[1]

Paul captures all of that in six words: *do the work of an evangelist*. There's some serious freight loaded into those six words. Let's bust open the crate and take a peek.[2]

Do . . .

Great word. *Do*. It's a verb, filled with action and intention. In the Greek here it forms a command, insisting that our vision of calling march toward mission. I love it because it takes evangelism and the called man and connects them through a work order. That's what I need: no-nonsense direction telling me what hill to take.

Yes, prayer for the lost is important. Every pastor should pray for the lost. But that's not what this passage is commanding. We're being summoned to do it. Strategizing on how the church can be more evangelistic is essential as well, but that's not what this is talking about. It's not about advising or lecturing or reading about it. It's simpler than that. Just do it.

I have to admit, I'm more comfortable "doing" other pastoral stuff. To me, almost anything's easier than doing evangelism. Visiting is easier, counseling is easier, leadership is easier, doing the abstinence talk to teens is easier. When it comes to doing evangelism, it's amazing how the unholy trinity—the world, the flesh, and the Devil—converge to keep me on the couch. But notice it doesn't say, "*feel* the work of an evangelist," or "*ponder* the work of an evangelist," or "affirm" or "encourage"; and certainly not "avoid the work of an evangelist." No, it's definitely "do." Anything less than "do" puts a man on the couch in potato position. And there are enough of us here already, thank you very much.

Doing involves going. Doing the work of evangelism puts pastors in motion. It couples the pastor to the Great Commission by pushing him out of the church and into circulation.

During England's civil war, Oliver Cromwell's troops faced a shortage of precious metals to help the war effort. Cromwell sent them to search the land—they needed to find metal somewhere. Word eventually reached him that the only available metal was in statues of saints in the churches. Cromwell delivered his now famous reply: "Well, melt down the saints and put them in circulation."[3] And so they did.

That's a picture of what I think God intends to do with the pastor. He melts the heart of the man for the lost and puts the summoned saint into circulation. And something wonderful results: as he reaches out to unbelievers, he starts to see the world differently. Needs become real. Fallenness is felt. Compassion flows with proclamation. The gospel becomes connected to the real world outside the pastor's study.

God sent his Son to us. God sends pastors into the world. If you don't want to reach people with the gospel, you're probably not called to be a pastor. Pastors *do* the work of evangelism.

. . . .

Doing the work of evangelism puts pastors in motion.

. . . .

Now if preaching is a pastoral priority (and it is), then doing the work of an evangelist overflows into our preaching. This is where the lost come to us. God loves the world so much that he agitates some right into a Sunday service. There they sit, uncomfortable, disoriented, and afraid to make some protocol mistake in front of a bunch of religious people. But they're right there, having voluntarily surrendered their time long enough to hear what you have to say. What will they hear from you?

Part of doing the work of an evangelist means preaching evangelistically. That doesn't mean every message is for the lost and begins and ends with an altar call. I can think of no better way to lose sheep than becoming a shepherd who never speaks to the flock!

Preaching evangelistically means something far more fruitful. It means the called man must commit to a future where he prepares messages not for meetings but for people. Most of his hearers will be saved; some will not.

A good pastor's voice reaches both the church and the world. From his opening comments to his points of application, he acknowledges the unbeliever's presence and seeks ports of entry where the gospel can be harbored. He never compromises; he conveys the truth. But he does it in a manner that says, "I can identify with your life and struggles." If that sounds difficult, it's because it is. But a called man has the capacity to do it. More than that, he's commanded to do it.

The Work . . .

Here's an interesting word choice for Paul: *work*. The Greek word for work means, well, *work*! Activity, labor, initiative—it's all included. In other words, like that enlightening experience with my college loan sharks, good intentions don't cut it. Evangelism has to show up in the way we do life and ministry.

To do the work we have to make it a priority. For pastors this is pretty huge. Let's face it. Shepherds tend their sheep. They're not wired to look outside the fold. And Lord knows there are enough problems in the sheepfold to keep a normal pastor swamped in ministry. For most pastors, this means making a priority of something that never seems to pop up on the screen of our lives. That's sure how it is for me.

· · · · · · · · · · · · · · · ·

Work to get outside; work to cultivate relationships; work to get into the community.

· · · · · · · · · · · · · · · ·

I wake up every morning next to my Christian wife and drive to an office full of Christians. I have meetings there with other Christians in which we talk about how to help Christians to be better Christians. I sit down in front of my Christian computer and write Christian e-mails to other Christians. I guess what I'm trying to say is that the only thing that's going to put me in front of unbelievers is a raging office fire that delivers unbelieving firemen to our building. Or I can *work*. Work to get outside; work to cultivate relationships; work to get into the community; work to do the work of an evangelist! That's the beauty of this command. It fixes the outward in our life and positions us to model it for the church.

Last year I took a class at a local college. One reason I did this was to connect with what the lost are thinking about these days. So I ended up sitting right behind a girl who introduced herself as an atheistic lesbian. We don't get many of those in our elders meetings. It was pure joy getting to know her. Eventually I was even able to talk about the gospel with her. But it took some work. I still ponder what she was telling her friends about me. Freaks me out a little bit.

But we don't just adjust our personal priorities. We build a church with biblical priorities. Evangelistic pastors build balanced churches. What does that mean? Here's how we say it at Four Oaks Community Church, where I presently pastor: "Four Oaks exists to treasure, grow, and go in the gospel of Jesus Christ." *Treasure* is the upward dimension, *grow* is the inward dimension, and *go* is the outward dimension. A healthy church blends the upward, outward, and inward emphases without allowing any one focus to co-opt the church. "We should beware," says Grudem, "of any attempts to reduce the purpose of the church to only one of these three and to say that it should be our primary focus."[4]

One of the things we tried to do in the last church where I pastored was to push the work of evangelism into every sphere of ministry in which we served. For example, those who had counseling responsibility established that discerning a potential evangelistic opportunity was their top priority in counseling. The church supported this evangelism priority. It wasn't uncommon for a pastor to call a member with whom he had an appointment to say, "Can I reschedule our time? I have an opportunity, if I can free the time up today, to meet with someone who doesn't know Jesus." No one ever said, "Hey, wait a minute. I'm a member! I got here first!" The pastors also went out regularly to local areas where people gathered, just to share the gospel. These are small steps we took to do the work of an evangelist.

There's one last thing I want to convey here. Suppose you find yourself someday as a pastor of a growing church. But as you walk around and talk to people, you're having a hard time running into anybody who's a new believer. You're growing, but not adding folks coming out of the world. So where are your new folks coming from? Probably the church down the street.

Studies show that much of the church growth that goes on today comes from saint-swapping—the movement of believers from one church to the next. I'm not saying that unattached Christians—and there are plenty around—can't be a legitimate target for church planters and outreach strategies. But when church plants or established churches grow at the expense of other gospel-preaching churches, is Christ's kingdom really advancing? In his book *Stealing Sheep*, William Chadwick observes, "The shifting of saints from one church to another is killing the church."[5] And let me get a little real here. If you build a church with somebody else's people, someday you'll be the somebody else who gets left for the next new thing.

But by cultivating and transferring a work ethic toward the lost (the outward dimension), we build stable churches where growth includes conversions. When pastoral effectiveness includes evangelism, the measure of local church success will include conversions. Folks who study this stuff will tell you that if you want to have cultural impact in your area, then you need to have a quarter of your growth from conversions.[6] I don't know how they measure these things, but what's lost if we make it a goal? Nothing but a little free time.

Australian pastors Colin Marshall and Tony Payne remind us, "Evangelism is at the heart of pastoral ministry. Ministry is not about just dealing with immediate crises or problems, or about building numbers, or about reforming structures. It's fundamentally about preparing souls for death."[7]

Of an Evangelist

"*Evangelist*: a bringer of good tidings; used of those who herald the gospel."[8] Definitions like this are helpful for the work, because they function like a work order. We don't just do, and we don't just work. We have a particular job. We're bringers, heralds of the gospel. This may seem obvious, but it's worth punctuating. The evangelist isn't just a man in motion doing good deeds or telling moral stories with an uplifting twist. He's a herald of a particular message: the gospel.

Have you ever thought about what it will be like to be a pastor and walk around in the world that way? In some traditions, you wear a collar that tells everybody you work for God (at least I think that's what it means). I don't wear a collar. I do sometimes wear a hoodie, though. In my hoodie I can live my entire life outside my church with no reference to the fact that I carry the most important message in the history of the universe. And if I just think of myself as a pastor to my flock, I can convince myself that whatever I do outside the church is private time. But to do the work of an evangelist is to live inside and outside the church as if you're one word away from a life-changing encounter every moment of your life.

. . . .

Live . . . as if you're one word away from a life-changing encounter every moment of your life.

. . . .

If you have no idea how to do this, watch a pastor who does the work of an evangelist. I like watching my friend Jim. Jim and I served on the same pastoral team for over 15 years. One thing we have in common is a fondness for eating out. But the way we look at the experience is pretty different. For me, being at a restaurant has an obvious goal: don't regret what you chose on the menu. Not for Jim. No sir, lunch meetings morph into a community experience for him. He glides through the restaurant shaking hands, meeting folks, and kissing babies. If restaurants held elections, Jim would be mayor for life.

When I talk to a waiter I have two questions: "What's the best thing you make?" and "Can you supersize it?" I think if I wasn't there, Jim would forget to order. He's too busy talking to the waiter and getting a personal history, a soul update, and any prayer needs. Leaving typically involves an invitation to church and maybe even plans to vacation together. And more often than not that unsuspecting waiter will have heard something about the Savior from Jim—something that might just save him or her from hell.

Now I'm convinced that Jim would be this way whether or not he was a pastor. But I love how Jim is happy to use the fact that he's a pastor to engage unbelievers. He likes the way it can throw them off balance, and he's good at disarming misconceptions. He finds that talking about being a pastor is a great door into talking about his Savior.

Many think Jim is just fearless, and that's why he's effective. But he clarifies that the work of an evangelist will often involve the presence of fear. He says:

> I used to think that if I just keep doing evangelism, eventually the fears would go away. But that hasn't been my experience, at least not the last twenty-one years (and I'm not holding my breath that it will change). I've learned that evangelism isn't about sharing the gospel so often that all fears are erased. I've been fearful every time I've opened my mouth to share the good news. What I've learned is that evangelism is about overcoming my fears and sharing the gospel despite the uncertainty. We're called to proclaim the good news and leave the results to God. And what a privilege it is to share the greatest news the world has ever heard.

I'm not Jim, but I sure thank God for him. He works hard to overcome fear and obey God. He works hard to do the work of an evangelist.

Getting Started

Maybe you think you're called but are feeling a little weak in this area of evangelism. How do you get started on "the work"?

Go with your story. I've never met an evangelist who wasn't deeply affected by his own conversion. He remembers . . . often. The good news remains glorious. That inspires me, because pastors must remember too. I'm not talking about just sharing your testimony. Stoke your love for the lost by remembering that you were lost at one time. You have the good news; they need to hear it. All that's missing is a connection point.

Look for opportunities. You didn't want to hear the good news until God sovereignly opened your heart to it. Who's to say the next person you talk to won't be where you were when you first heard the message of salvation? Remember, God created us in Christ Jesus for good works that are already prepared (Eph. 2:10). Isn't that cool? The opportunities are already there for those who do the work of an evangelist.

Build relationships. As much as we would love to have that restaurant conversion testimony to share with the folks at home, our greatest impact will more likely be the slow and patient sowing of gospel seed in the routine of life. The people we see week in and week out—that's our field. We're not just downloading truth; we're loving people. Our approach must be as gracious as the news we carry. Find a called man, and you should discover a network of unbelievers he's reaching.

One Great Object: Win Souls

Charles Spurgeon trained men called to ministry. He had a lecture titled "On Conversion As Our Aim." Think about how his words fit into your vision for pastoral ministry:

Our great object of glorifying God is to be mainly achieved by the winning of souls. We must see souls born unto God. If we do not, our cry should be that of Rachel, "Give me children, or I die." If we do not win souls we should mourn as the husbandman who sees no harvest, as the fisherman who returns to his cottage with an empty net, or as the huntsman who has in vain roamed over hill and dale . . . The ambassadors for peace should not cease to weep bitterly until sinners weep for their sins.[9]

If Spurgeon's words reflect genuine emotions you've experienced to some degree in looking out on the world around you, then rejoice that God's grace has already begun forming within you a heart for the lost. And if those three "getting started" steps I just mentioned—going with your story, looking for evangelism opportunities, building relationships with unbelievers—ring true in your mind and heart as habits you feel compelled to pursue, that's worth your deepest gratitude to God as well.

All those things could be important evidence in determining whether you've been summoned to the ministry of the gospel as you actively wrestle with this question: *Do you love the lost?*

For Additional Study

The Gospel and Personal Evangelism, Mark Dever

The Heart of Evangelism, Jerram Barrs

Marks of the Messenger, J. Mack Stiles

Evangelism & the Sovereignty of God, J. I. Packer

Salvation to the Ends of the Earth, Andreas J. Köstenberger and Peter T. O'Brien

A Summons Story
John Bunyan: A Calling Confirmed by the Church[1]

It was a pitiful group gathered around the bed of the dying John Gifford. He had been the faithful pastor of a small congregation trying to survive in uncertain times. Now he lay gasping for breath, seeking to be faithful to his flock to the very end. Among his last few words on earth was this plea: *"Spend much time before the Lord about choosing a pastor."*

All the while, his eyes were fixed on a young man in the group. Rough around the edges, the focus of Gifford's gaze was a newer Christian. Nothing in his background indicated he was fit for the Lord's service. He was a tradesman, and wanted to stay that way.

But God had other plans for John Bunyan. Almost in spite of himself, he was thrust into opportunities where his public testimony produced remarkable fruit. His church took notice. Bunyan tells of it:

> For after I had been about five or six years awakened, and helped myself to see both the want and worth of Jesus Christ our Lord, and also enabled to venture my soul upon Him, some of the most able among the saints with us, I say the most able for judgment and holiness of life, as they conceived, did perceive that God had counted me worthy to understand something of His will in His holy and blessed Word, and had given me utterance, in some measure, to express what I saw to others for edification; therefore they desired me, and that with much earnestness, that I would be willing, at sometimes, to take in hand, in one of the meetings, to speak a word of exhortation unto them.[2]

The church wisely tested the fledgling preacher, giving him opportunities to preach. Though continually encouraged by the congregation, Bunyan was, at best, a reluctant minister.

Then one day, he read the words of Paul in 1 Corinthians 16, exhorting the gifted to be devoted to the service of the saints. These words gave weight to the encouragement from his church, convincing Bunyan to stop running from his call:

> By this text I was made to see that the Holy Ghost never intended that men who have gifts and abilities should bury them in the earth, but rather did command and stir up such to the exercise of their gift, and also did commend those that were apt and ready so to do. Wherefore, though of myself of all the saints the most unworthy, yet I, but with great fear and trembling at the sight of my own weakness, did set upon the work, and did according to my gift, and the proportion of my faith, preach that blessed gospel that God had showed me in the holy Word of Truth.[3]

Bunyan entered into the ministry through the identification and exhortation of a small congregation who had to scrounge for places to meet. As the persecution in Restoration England descended across the countryside, the fragile little flock went underground. And the man Gifford hoped would care for them went to prison.

For a total of twelve years, Bunyan languished in Bedford Jail. But as we know now, he was an extraordinarily busy prisoner. It was during this time that he wrote his autobiography, *Grace Abounding to the Chief of Sinners*, and, of course, *Pilgrim's Progress*. Bunyan didn't write from jail to fill his time or buy his freedom; he wrote because God had called him to the ministry, the church had affirmed the call, and he wasn't going to let a little thing like persecution keep him from doing what he was called to do. He wrote to *pastor*—and God's church has been fed by his ministry from those days forward.

9

Who Agrees?

· · · · · · · · · · · · · · · ·

Remember my story from chapter 1? There I am, a guy with a lot of zeal and a growing sense that I'm supposed to somehow, someday be in ministry. I had no training or preparation; only an intense ambition to preach the Bible. Was that aspiration enough?

Meanwhile, back at the ranch . . . well, I was just trying to get by—to build a marriage, keep a job, pay down college debt, match my socks each morning. Along the way, I had several people telling me they saw some potential for pastoral ministry. And they weren't even my mother. Did that somehow complete the launch sequence on my summons? What should I do next? Contact a mission agency? Search for a seminary? Just step out in faith and start a church? Or was there something else, something more I should be looking for?

If you've made it this far, you must have some sense that God is doing a work in your heart. There's some kind of summoning going on. So now we've got to talk about what to do with it.

A Threefold Cord

As I look at Scripture, survey a bit of church history, and observe what happens to men who cross over into pastoral ministry, there are three entwined cords that bind a man to his call. Each thread strengthens the summons. These are his internal call, his preparation, and his confirmation by others—a threefold cord of calling. These aren't consecutive steps; rather, they're three independent strands that come together in God's providence to help the summons find its fulfillment.

Cord #1: Internal Calling

Ask any man in ministry about how he got there, and he'll have a story about something going on inside him. Sometimes it's a sudden, watershed experience, receiving what Spurgeon described as "a yearning, a pining, a famishing to proclaim the Word."[1] For other men it's kind of a creeping call; it sneaks up almost unnoticed, until one day the man awakens to discover the call has taken up residence like an unexpected squatter.

Much of this book has been about the internal calling. We've seen how a man's call to ministry is embedded in his call to salvation. It all starts there—awakening us, defining us, transforming us. It's the most important thing about every believer; but some believers are summoned into leadership among God's people. There's something they get from God, you might say, that makes them want to shepherd God's people and preach God's Word. The internal call involves character, gifting, preaching capabilities, a heart to care, and a love for the lost. For a man being summoned to ministry, this internal sense of call must be compelling and enduring, lasting for as long as he's in ministry.

Cord #2: Preparation

Okay, this is an important one. It's so important that we'll devote the book's final chapter to it. Why? Because you need to know what to do during those months or years when you carry an internal call but wait for confirmation. Preparation is way more than just killing time. We all have this tendency to think the inner sense should be fast-tracked—punch the accelerator and go for it. And if other people happen to recognize something in us? Pedal to the floor and look out for cops. But there's no avoiding the yield signs and yellow lights of preparation.

I had an internal call long before anyone else saw it. Boy, did I think they were slow! Eventually I did get some encouragement from others—God bless 'em. But they were encouraging a guy who was rather . . . umm, undeveloped. (Discerning observers might have said "proud" or "clueless," but let's just go with unprepared.)

But you know what? I'm so glad I didn't run immediately through the doors that seemed to be opening early in my Christian life. And just as grateful, I think, are those upon whom I would have imposed my unprepared self.

Maybe you can relate. You humbly realize you need preparation. We'll get to that soon. But before we get there, we need to discuss the grace of external confirmation.

Cord #3: External Confirmation

This is where we'll spend the bulk of this chapter. Let me start with a simple definition: *External confirmation is the process of evaluation whereby the church affirms God's call to the man.* Think of it this way. A personal sense is never enough to propel a man into ministry. The subjective sense of calling must be objectively validated. External assessment is an essential cord that tethers you, and your church, to safety.

Why Confirmation?

Why is this kind of assessment and validation from others needed? First, because it's a biblical principle. The biblical record presents some wonderful and diverse examples of how external confirmation plays out.

Now before you read about Moses and start looking for sparks in every bush, just a heads up—be careful about drawing too much from Old Testament examples like Moses, David, and the prophets who received their callings from God himself for specific redemptive purposes.

· · · · · · · · · · · · · · · ·

The inner call stirring the soul is validated by a confirmation external to the man.

· · · · · · · · · · · · · · · ·

But we can still glean important things from those stories. Throughout the history of Israel, there's a practice of anointing and acclamation. It represents a public recognition that God is summoning a man for his purposes. Even Jesus submits himself to baptism, which proves to be a moment of confirmation for his public ministry. At the end of his ministry, Jesus, in various ways, commissions his disciples for the work of the gospel— most notably in the discourses of John 13–17 and in the Great Commission (Matt. 28:18–20). So when the disciples turn into first-generation church planters, they're operating with a deep sense of having been sent by another. What we glean from this biblical pattern is that the inner call stirring the soul is validated by a confirmation external to the man.

This intertwining of internal call and external confirmation is clarified in one of the few books on pastoral ministry that fall into the must-read category for any man sensing a summons. *The Christian Ministry* by Charles Bridges is near the top of my list of such books. Bridges was a British Anglican pastor who linked arms with Charles Spurgeon, J. C. Ryle, and other bold men of God to build gospel-preaching churches in Victorian England. *The Christian Ministry* explodes with insight for pastors at all points of ministry life. On the matter of calling, Bridges nails it as he carefully explains both the subjective aspect—"a desire for the work"—plus an objective one—"fitness for the office":[2]

> Our authority is derived conjointly from God and from the Church—that is, originally from God—confirmed through the medium of the Church. The external call is a commission received from and recognized by the Church, according to the sacred and primitive order; not indeed qualifying the Minister, but accrediting him, whom God had internally and suitably qualified. This call communicates therefore only official authority. The internal call is the voice and power of the Holy Ghost, directing the will and the judgment, and conveying personal qualifications. Both calls, however—though essentially distinct in their character and source—are indispensable for the exercise of our commission.[3]

Bridges is pointing to God's sovereign activity in both

internal and external calls. It's not like the internal call comes from God and the external comes from man. No, God works through people in both cases. In the internal call God works through the human agency of our own will and judgment; in the external call he works through the human agency of his church.

Who Confirms?

Who weighs out the external confirmation? It comes from two sources.

Primarily, Church Leaders

Confirmation involves examination: "and let them also be tested first" (1 Tim. 3:10). Paul pronounces this prerequisite for deacons actually, but it should be assumed for elders as well. That's why the elder requirements exist in the Pastoral Epistles. If you want to church-plant or pastor, bring a #2 pencil. There's a test.

Testing is administered by those in authority—at least that's what it meant back in my high school. Hey, I would have loved to take tests conducted by my fellow students. That would have certainly put me on the honor roll. But I was stuck with the old-fashioned rule that teachers conduct tests. Why teachers? It's this crazy idea that teachers were somehow more qualified than guys like me who slept through class and viewed detention as an AP class. Now I get it. And it's an important aspect of understanding your call. External confirmation must come from someone who's qualified.

You see this principle working out in Antioch, a model first-century church. When the Caller calls Barnabas and Saul, he speaks to the entire leadership team, saying, "Gentlemen, your attention please! Set apart these two for the work I've called them to" (Acts 13:2, my rough version).

It's interesting—he's not speaking directly to Barnabas and Saul, but to the others about them. The other leaders were asked to affirm and send these men. Let's set aside Saul for a moment, who received his internal call complete with an appearance of Christ himself. What about Barnabas? Up to this point we know he's a faithful man in the church. He's so much of an encourager that, well, this becomes his name. He's demonstrated his commitment by giving heroically to the cause (Acts 4:36–37). He's a discerning and courageous man, recognizing the call on Saul's life when others don't and willing to stand with him (Acts 9:26–27). In Acts 11:22–24, we find that he's a "good man, full of the Holy Spirit and of faith." He's evidently got the goods to preach, but we don't really know what formal ministry position he held.

· · · · · · · · · · · · · · · ·

Their emergence into ministry was a holy setting-apart by other leaders, not an ambitious stepping-out.

· · · · · · · · · · · · · · · ·

So you get to Acts 13 and you have two guys. One guy's call is pronounced, but he has been laboring in relative obscurity. The other guy's call is revealed in service, slowly, over time. Both Saul and Barnabas positioned themselves to be known, evaluated, and equipped under God-ordained leadership. Barnabas was sent to Antioch by the Jerusalem church; Saul was brought to Antioch by Barnabas. Both labored in concert with other leaders in the local church. They weren't free-agent apostles looking for "sponsors" or "ministry partners." Their prior activity was largely in preparation and in service to the church where they belonged. When they were confirmed to ministry, it was as "known men." Their emergence into ministry was a holy setting-apart by other leaders, not an ambitious stepping-out. They honored God and served the church by waiting for external confirmation of their internal call. This becomes the pattern of the New Testament church: elders are called by God and confirmed by leaders.[4]

Secondarily, the Church Itself

Think about what we've learned already from 1 Timothy 3 and Titus 1. God gives specific qualities as a sign of the summons. But in a real sense the whole church is part of the confirmation process. You live and minister among folks who know you and have opinions about you. If you're a saint in front of the elders and a jerk to everybody else, your chances of confirmation are microscopic. Now, the goal isn't to live your life auditioning for the ministry. It's to live your life loving God and others in a way that will increasingly affect people in the way a pastor should affect them.

Let's get more specific. Consider just some of the requirements in these passages: a pastor must be above reproach (1 Tim. 3:2; Titus 1:6–7), respectable (1 Tim. 3:2), gentle (1 Tim. 3:3), well thought of by outsiders (1 Tim. 3:7), and hospitable (Titus 1:8). These qualities by definition involve other people. In fact, the only way to truly apply these passages is by soliciting the perspective of the church.

Confirmation from the Qualified

A personal sense of calling, though vital, is never enough to propel a man into ministry. There must be confirmation, not only by those who have the responsibility and authority to render it, but also from church members. They need to be able to see you one day as their pastor. So the question is, in your life, who occupies that position of bringing confirmation? If you don't know the answer to this question you're in danger of falling into Sisco's summons.

Meet Reverend Cassidy, or Sisco to his friends. Sisco is a licensed minister of the Universal Life Church, which boasts over seventeen million members worldwide. According to the ULC's ministerial records, Sisco is now qualified to officiate at weddings, conduct funerals, and perform baptisms. However, the baptisms are a bit difficult since Reverend Sisco Cassidy has an incurable fear of water.

This might seem strange unless you're aware that dear Reverend Cassidy is a cat! It appears that Sisco's seemingly bored and cynical owner saw an advertisement by the ULC asking for leaders to start a new congregation. Apparently concerned about a potential shortage in ministers, Sisco's owner sponsored his cat, and Sisco was shortly thereafter ordained as a minister in the ULC with all rights thereunto. I understand that shortly after this, Sisco took up golf.

Sisco's ministry isn't as bizarro as it seems. I had a pastor friend tell me about a couple who wanted to get married, but the church wouldn't perform the ceremony. Since they didn't want to go the justice-of-the-peace route, they simply had the father of the bride get an online ordination, and he did their ceremony.

Sisco's owner-appointed path is easy—but it's not biblical. Your call to ministry must be confirmed by qualified people. Charles Bridges wisely observes that "ministerial failure" can sometimes be traced back to the moment a man first entered the work. Bridges asks, "Was the call to the sacred office clear *in the order of the church*, and according to the will of God?"[5]

What Does This Mean for You?

What difference does this matter of external confirmation of leadership really make? What good does it do—for you personally, and for God's people together?

You're Protected

The church's role in confirming the call protects the office of ministry from corrupted ambitions. But it's meant to do more than that. External confirmation gives a man confidence that he isn't deceiving himself about his qualifications for ministry.[6] It allows him to step into the authority of his office having already proved himself, thus freeing him to do the work of ministry rather than the work of campaigning for people's allegiance. And it establishes a secure relationship between people and leader. Everyone involved knows there's external evaluation and oversight to a man's leadership and the church's response to that leadership. The called man of God can then "go forward within the fellowship and under the guidance of the Church."[7]

God's Church Is Protected

Think about this: My call isn't *my* call; it's God's call to his church. It's not just about us; it's about the lives of those we lead—or at least are trying to lead. Putting a man in a pulpit when he's neither called or gifted to be there is a disaster in the making.

Mr. Spurgeon certainly understood this. He wrote, "It is a fearful calamity to a man to miss his calling, and to the church upon whom he imposes himself, his mistake involves an affliction of the most grievous kind."[8]

Too many men have made this grievous mistake. Take T. J., for example. T. J.'s conversion was so dramatic that he naturally assumed God had big plans for him. As a strong man with a strong personality, he was surely capable of being as productive in vocational ministry as in the firm. Or so he thought. At church, T. J.'s outspoken manner and crisply expressed opinions were regularly mistaken for evidence of a call to preach. Friends began encouraging him to plant a church.

• • • • • • • • • • • • • • • •

He could never figure out what was wrong . . .
but he never expended much brain power on it.

• • • • • • • • • • • • • • • •

Time passed, and T. J.—stinging over the fact that he hadn't yet been formally asked to plant a church—became frustrated.

His denomination's leadership just didn't seem to appreciate his gift or know how to utilize his style of leadership. Meanwhile, T. J.'s pastors were noticing some deficiencies in his marriage. Yet their appeals fell on deaf ears. T. J. just thought they were unsupportive and a bit too narrow in the way they evaluated men. T. J. wanted impact; they were appealing for process.

Eventually T. J. left the church and enrolled in Bible school, completing the program in record time. After graduation, he started a church in the city where he'd grown up. But there were problems from the start. The core group was a collision of personalities that never settled into a team. T. J. could never figure out what was wrong with the team, but he never expended much brain power on it; he was drawn to projects more than people.

As for the Sunday meetings, the messages tended to go long—T. J. had so much to say! However, guests who came seldom returned more than once or twice, if at all. When asked why, they would allude to something about the preacher that just hit them wrong.

Soon the unique pressures of church planting revealed the cracks in T. J.'s marriage. Conflict at home became more frequent and intense. His wife began to show signs of emotional withdrawal.

The gossip started, the core team unraveled, people left, funding tanked, and finally T. J. fled. He was exhausted, angry, and just wanted out. Now he's selling real estate and refuses to attend church at all.

There are hundreds of tragic stories like this—legacies of unchecked ambition. The drive of men like T. J. downgrades the input of others. It claims the right to self-appointment and self-anointing, the unilateral definition of one's own call. Armed with desire, intelligence, and drive, too many people leap to the self-serving conclusion that these are the only attributes God requires.

The Bible teaches otherwise. As Oswald Sanders asked, "Should it not be the office that seeks the man, rather than the man the office?"[9]

You Need Others

Are there people close enough to you to see if you have the gifting, character, and live up to the requirements to aspire to pastoral ministry?

God has configured the body in such a way that none of us can fully perceive the extent or the grace of our own gifts. God has done this intentionally, so we might be dependent upon one another. We need other people to understand the direction and the momentum of our calling.

This was wonderfully expressed by Charles Spurgeon upon accepting the call to the pastorate of New Park Street Church in London (at age twenty!):

> I sought not to come to you, for I was a minister of an obscure but affectionate people. I never solicited advancement. The first note of invitation from your deacons came quite unlooked-for, and I trembled at the idea of preaching in London. I could not understand how it had come about, and even now I am filled with astonishment at the wondrous Providence. I would wish to give myself into the hands of our covenant God, whose wisdom directs all things. He shall choose for me; and so far as I can judge, this is his choice.[10]

In embracing the value of an external call, the summoned man puts himself in a position, like Spurgeon, to be "filled with astonishment at the wondrous Providence" of God. The called man says to the believers and leaders around him, "I'll trust your estimation more than my own. I'll trust that God will speak not only to me, but also through you to me. And I submit my sense of trajectory to that process—knowing that when it's complete, it will speak far more clearly and strongly than any conviction I come to on my own."

As I look back twenty-six years to that summoning season of my life, I see more clearly how God was working out his perfect plan in a perfect way at his perfect time. That's not to say I didn't struggle; few men are spared the experience of uncertainty. The struggle with uncertainty is part of the package. But there's no uncertainty in God. He's the Craftsman of our call. He weaves the cords of inner call, preparation, and confirmation and lashes you to the mast as you set sail for uncharted waters.

· · · · · · · · · · · · · · · ·

Find some way to get people close enough to you to be part of the adventure of external confirmation.

· · · · · · · · · · · · · · · ·

So guys, if you find yourself alone with a sense of call, check your deodorant. No matter what your ecclesiology and polity might be, you should be able to find some way to get people close enough to you to be part of the adventure of external confirmation.

As we walk the road toward ministry, we begin to discover

that God wants us to arrive in ministry having learned valuable lessons necessary for effective ministry. They're lessons that require trust in God. They make *our* church more important than *my* ministry.

That's why, concerning any man who may be called to gospel ministry, we should ask, *Who agrees?*

For Additional Study
The Christian Ministry, Charles Bridges
Test, Train, Affirm, and Send into Ministry, Brian Croft
Called to the Ministry, Edmund P. Clowney

A Summons Story
John Newton: Knowing the Value of Waiting[1]

Miscellaneous Thoughts and Enquiries Upon an Important Subject—sounds like a college term paper—and a boring one at that. But this wasn't the random notes of an inquisitive mind musing over theoretical topics. It was a journal of six weeks of sober, exhausting heart examination—the self-study of a man desperate to hear from God.

John Newton was thirty-three. He'd already lived a full life, staring death in the face numerous times and doing daring and dastardly things most people never imagined. And now it had come to this. A convert of only a few short years, recently retired from the abomination of slave trading, Newton could not help wondering if he was called to ministry.

He emerged from his six-week sabbatical fully convinced he was called to gospel ministry. The only questions were where and how. Newton was decidedly older than most aspirants, nearly all of whom stepped into clergy life straight from school. Moreover, the traditional route for a man was to apply for ordination in the Church of England. Yet there were also new opportunities outside the established church—exciting, but risky independent works.

From the get-go, Newton's path into ministry was strewn with obstacles. The first was a thorny one. The people Newton believed he was supposed to join (the Anglicans) didn't want him; yet he sensed no calling toward the people who did want him (the Independents).

Newton's answer to his call turned out to be a six-year wandering in uncertainty and opposition. He sought the counsel of those who knew him well, including his wife and family. These counselors helped convince him that his vision for ministry would best be served in the established church. He dutifully worked through the various tests and requirements for ordination. But he was rejected. And rejected again. And again. The reasons were perplexing—he hadn't attended the right schools, he was too "enthusiastic," his sinful past wasn't fitting for a man of the cloth.

All told, Newton was rejected six times from the ministry he sought to pursue. He just had to wait. He carried a confidence in God and the resilience of a man who had faced far worse than discrimination. So he went into preparation mode: *For the present I must remain as I am and endeavor to be as useful as I can in private life until I can see farther.*[2]

God used that waiting time to solidify a man who wasn't nearly as stable as he thought when he emerged from his six-week seclusion with his summons. Years later, in a letter to a young man in a similar predicament, Newton reveals the value of waiting in his life:

> It is very difficult to restrain ourselves within the bounds of prudence here, when our zeal is warm, a sense of the love of Christ is upon our hearts, and a tender compassion for perishing sinners is ready to prompt us to break out too soon—but "he who believes shall not make haste."
>
> I was about five years under this constraint. Sometimes I thought I must preach, though it was in the streets. I listened to everything that seemed plausible, and to many things that were not so. But the Lord graciously, and as it were insensibly, hedged up my way with thorns; otherwise, if I had been left to my own spirit, I would have put it quite out of my power to have been brought into such a sphere of usefulness, as he in his good time has been pleased to lead me to.
>
> And I can now see clearly, that at the time I would first have gone out, though my intention was, I hope, good in the main—yet

I overrated myself, and had not that spiritual judgment and experience which are requisite for so great a service.[3]

Time well spent prepared Newton for so great a service. Newton came to understand that a period of waiting is part of God's perfect timing.

PART THREE

Waiting

· · · · · · · · · · · · · · · ·

10

While You Wait

· · · · · · · · · · · · · · · ·

You're sitting in the movie theater, lost in the unfolding saga filling the screen in front of you. One hand is buried in a gihugic tub of popcorn, the other locked like a vice on a gallon of Coke. You're no longer in your seat; you've been transported into the scene—piloting the spacecraft through galaxies unknown, or careening that vintage muscle car through city streets, the bad guys right on your tail. And that dude in the dark stair-well oblivious to the fact he's about to get whacked in a cruelly inventive way? You're right behind him. All you can hear is the sound of breathing—is it his or yours?

Suddenly a cell phone rings. Two rings later you realize this isn't part of the movie—it's your phone and you're an idiot. Conscious that *you* are now in danger of getting whacked in a cruelly inventive way by adjacent theater patrons, you fish for the phone, hit the silencer, and look to see who called. And . . . bummer. Turns out it's the call you've been waiting for—the company letting you know whether you got the job, or the girl from church letting you know if she's interested in that coffee date. But you're in a dark theater and can't answer the phone.

Sometimes you get a call that might just change your life. It's the right call, you're the right guy—but under the circumstances you can't take it. Right number, right guy, wrong time.

You have to wait.

The Paradox of Preparation

We've emphasized in this book that the impetus behind the call to plant or pastor originates within the mind and intention of an all-wise, all-knowing, all-sovereign God. In spite of our frequently me-centered approach to spirituality, God doesn't need us. For *anything*. He's self-sufficient, without need of anything outside himself for his subsistence or satisfaction. If he didn't need to create us in the first place, he certainly doesn't need us as leaders.

And yet, in his grace, God does summon men, one by one, to plant churches and pastor his people. So, where are you in this matter of the summons?

My guess is you're in one of two places. Reading this book has amped your vision for pastoral ministry, and you're just looking for a "what next?" Your summons seems crystal clear, like the toll of a bell on a quiet winter morning. But there's another group, one more sobered by this book. You sense some clarity coming, but it's not a welcome arrival because it appears to challenge your dream. You felt called to pastor or plant a church, but now you have more questions about your suitability, about your call.

Regardless of where you are, I want to use this final chapter to pastor you. I want to give you some practical things to do to move toward the summons. But more importantly, I want to impart faith to you for God's good plan regardless of the outcome.

• • • • • • • • • • • • • • • •

God never gives a summons (or withholds one!)
without having a good plan behind it.

• • • • • • • • • • • • • • • •

You see, God never gives a summons (or withholds one!) without having a good plan behind it. Because he's a good God, all his plans are good. All calls have limits—limits of gifting and sphere and opportunity and time. So the goal of this chapter is to build your faith in God's abundant goodness and wisdom as he perfectly fits his man for the mission. Limits and all. In pastoral ministry, or outside it—wherever!

So what do you do now? One word: prepare!

Great, Dave. Nice touch. Thanks for the brevity.

Many guys wonder why God would give them such a strong desire for ministry but not open a door to satisfy it. I like to tell them to interpret that desire as a mandate to prepare. It's not a license to quit your job or plant a church, at least not yet. It's a call to prepare your soul, your life, and your mind for the joys and rigors of ministry. "The greatest and hardest preparation," says Bridges, "is within."[1]

Preparation for ministry can feel like a paradox. God calls you to start now, taking on certain tasks you wouldn't necessarily do apart from the summons. At the same time, God calls you to wait—to trust in him as months or years pass and *he* prepares *you* for pastoral ministry. You're taking action, while also waiting.

How do you do both? In this chapter we'll explore how to act and wait at the same time. Equally important, we'll look at how these steps can serve the man who ultimately realizes he isn't called to pastoral ministry.

Start Now

A man listening for a call is never a man sitting still. A key sign of the summons is godly ambition that's being channeled into action. That's why, as a leader responsible for weighing in on external call issues, I'm not just looking at who a guy is and what he might do. I'm looking for what he's already doing. That helps me gauge the degree of aspiration as well as desire— "If anyone *aspires* to the office of overseer, he *desires* a noble task" (1 Tim. 3:1).

Brothers, there's a lot you can do right now to prepare yourself in the summons. Here are some ideas to get you started. For each one, I've included some specific "next actions" you can take.

1. Be honest about your desires. If you "aspire to the office of overseer," tell your pastor. If you don't have a pastor, find a good church and get a pastor. It's not humble to remain silent about your dreams. You're not Mary treasuring "up all these things in [your] heart" (Luke 2:51). It's far more profitable to share your dreams. Evaluation from others is going to happen eventually; why not let it start now?

A practical step: Using some of the categories from this book, write your pastor and share your sense of call and desire for ministry. Invite him to lunch to specifically discuss his feedback on your letter.

2. *Pray*. Do you consistently pray about your calling?

A *practical step*: Schedule regular times of prayer, perhaps even personal retreats, where you're able to both stoke your sense of call and lay it on the altar before the Lord.

3. *Start serving*. Calling is revealed in service. A young, called guy so often wants to find a role *right now* that matches his gifts. But at this stage, the summons is not a warrant to flex your gifts; it's an invitation to be a servant wherever you're needed. Feel called to preach to the masses? Great—go teach in children's ministry. It's a great place to start.

A *practical step*: Go to your church leaders and say, "Where does our church need the most help?" Then do whatever they need you to do. Serving in obscurity can do more to shape a future leader than a dozen years of combing evangelicalism for the perfect position.

4. *If you're in college, pursue a vocational direction*. Moving directly from college into full-time ministry is the exception, not the rule. Don't assume you need a degree that will directly relate to ministry.

A *practical step*: Be a disciplined, well-balanced student. Pursue excellence and immerse yourself in the ministry opportunities that come with college life. Don't hide in your Christian group—engage the campus as a witness for Christ. Learn to think and persuade from a biblical perspective. Choose someone who you think is a humble influencer of others, and ask a lot of questions.

5. *Pursue counsel and evaluation*. Are you actively and consistently pursuing the wisdom of men who know you and your sense of call?

A practical step: Keep taking your pastor out to lunch—invite his ongoing insight into your personal life. Also, cultivate accountable fellowship with wise men your age and older.

6. *Study.* Are you deepening your theological well through a systematic study of sound doctrine and biblical theology?

A practical step: Ask your pastor for a book list to study. Then make a plan for how and when you'll complete that study—and give it to your pastor so he can follow up with you.

7. *Mature.* How does your life presently line up with the qualities of an elder as found in 1 Timothy and Titus? Where do you need to grow?

A practical step: Seek regular accountability and correction from those closest to you. If you're married, begin with your wife. As Wayne Grudem says, "It is not optional that [pastors'] lives be examples for others to follow; it is a requirement."[2]

8. *Get your house in order.* The path to pastoral ministry is often a sacrificial one. You may need to live lean and flexible. Are you prepared to make sacrifices to pursue your call? I know a number of men, for example, whose ability to act on an opportunity has been blocked by excessive debt. You should also care for your wife as you explore your call. Remember our earlier discussion of this—if you're called, she must confidently agree. If she doesn't, then preparing for ministry means hearing her reservations, carefully considering her reluctance, and humbly responding to her observations.

A practical step: Get rid of all the debt you can, and stay that way. If you're married, make sure your call is an open conversation your wife can have whenever she wants. Explore any concerns she may bring. Discuss any objections with trusted friends and a wise pastor.

9. *Patiently persevere.* Are you committed to waiting for God to bring you into ministry rather than anxiously brokering your own opportunities?

A practical step: Pursue a vocation that you can live on and grow in. Develop employable skills so you won't be depending on the ministry for survival.

· · · · · · · · · · · · · · · ·

There's a lot you can do right now to
prepare yourself in the summons.

· · · · · · · · · · · · · · · ·

Charles Spurgeon knew a little bit about getting men into ministry. He was all about getting men busy wanting and doing all they could for the kingdom. His advice is worth taking: "Qualify yourselves for larger spheres, you who are in little places; but do not neglect your studies to look after better positions. Be prepared for an opening when it comes, and rest assured that the office will come to the man who is fit for the office."[3]

Learn How to Wait

I've got a theory: I hate to wait, so God calls me to write. I'm serious. If you're an impatient, nonwaiting, quick-turnaround kind of guy, writing is like a bandit, snatching your cherished sense of progress and holding it hostage until you pay the ransom of time—time in rewrites, time in editing, time in research, downtime. Eventually—although it never seems soon enough—

you're rewarded with a growing manuscript. But in my world, there's no way to write quickly. It just takes time. Time is essential to the summons.

Whenever you see someone called in the Bible, God inserts a time variable into the equation. Take Abraham: promised a son at seventy-five, delivery at one hundred. Try Moses: forty years in the desert—twice. David gets to chill for about thirty years between anointing and ruling. Paul gets a little seventeen-year wait between calling and a broader recognition of his role.

Why so much time? Because God uses the passing of months and years to test a man and to sanctify him. All those requirements we've talked about in this book? They don't come as downloadable files. They're worked into a man over time.

· · · · · · · · · · · · · · · · ·

God uses the passing of months and years
to test a man and to sanctify him.

· · · · · · · · · · · · · · · · ·

The tests of time usually involve trials. There's the trial of waiting, and the other trials that just come with life. For the man called to the pastorate, there's always a dual purpose in these trials: to sanctify him as a believer, and to prepare him as a pastor.

This was expressed well by John Newton:

> When God intends a man for eminent usefulness in the ministry, he leads him through deep waters, and causes him to drink freely of the cup of spiritual sorrow, that he may be prepared, by a long course of afflictive experiences, to sympathize with

tempted and desponding believers; and may learn how to administer to them that consolation by which his own heart was at last comforted.[4]

More than anything, times of waiting and trials are meant to drive a man to confidence in the providence of God for himself and others. Providence—a theological term for God's active and benevolent sovereignty in the affairs of man—brings God's character and our life experiences together under the banner of Romans 8:28: "And we know that for those who love God all things work together for good, for those who are called according to his purpose." Simply put, God's providence is his proving himself good to us over time.

In Obscurity

My summons to ministry played out over a five-year period. Three of those years were spent working night shifts as a security guard in a hospital, for a little over minimum wage. It was honest labor, but in my mind it redefined the meaning of a dead-end job. I tried to get other jobs, but God kept me there. I was involved in a good church, learning to serve, getting settled in marriage, and experiencing the reality therapy of life outside of the cocoon of college. Waiting was my classroom, my proving ground, my assessment center. Waiting was God's good providence working for good in the life of a future pastor.

Time has another benefit for called men: it allows them to serve in obscurity. Brothers, we need obscurity. We need to do ministry without acclaim so that we won't be acclaim addicts when it comes. Anonymity is the ground from which pastors are harvested. Obscurity fertilizes the man with humility so that what he grows into can really bear fruit.

. . . .

Our sovereign God will not forget or
neglect the work he's doing in you,
or the place he's carving out for you.

. . . .

I've got a buddy named Brian. Brian was a news manager with NBC before going into pastoral ministry. His summons involved a long season of secret service—and I don't mean the kind that involves presidential motorcades and semiautomatic weapons. "Monday through Friday," Brian said, "I would oversee a newsroom staff of a hundred people and was responsible for millions of dollars' worth of bleeding-edge technology. But serving at church on Sunday, I was taking instruction from a guy who was *very particular* about the way I should coil a microphone cable."

Brian eventually left NBC to pursue theological training, and served fruitfully in ministry for twelve years. But he'll never forget how the lessons of obscurity prepared him for ministry. "Although I never saw the connection at the time," he says, "serving on sound team and in children's ministry became critical contexts where God worked in me before he worked through me as a pastor."

Maybe you've been patient for a long time, but nothing's happening. How long should you wait? Don't worry about time passing you by—our sovereign God will not forget or neglect the work he's doing in you, or the place he's carving out for you. God isn't playing with your future. He's fashioning you for it.

Here are some questions that will steady your soul over time.

- Do I recognize the hand of God, the Caller, in placing the burden of calling in my life?
- Do I trust that where I am in life today—no matter how far it is from where I think I should be—can never limit God's ability to accomplish his will in my life?
- Am I responding to my present situation with faith?
- Would others say I'm a grateful man?
- Do I trust God to both clarify my call and confirm his direction?
- Am I content with the process God has me in?
- Am I watching my doctrine and life closely (1 Tim. 4:16)?
- Am I investing in my own sanctification and in the deepening of my doctrine?
- Would others say I'm using this season of my life to its maximum benefit?

What If I'm Not Called?

I've been sobered to realize that this book will undoubtedly, to some extent, be an instrument of sorrow in some men's lives. Some will read it and realize with sadness that they've not received the summons to vocational ministry. Others, who thought they were within grasp of a long-desired call, will discover a gulf of inexperience, character deficiency, or independence that puts the realization of their dream out of reach—at least for now. And some will recognize that God in his providence has, for them, made that gulf permanently uncrossable.

Don't view this as God's opposition; see it as God's kind redirection. You're not alone.

Let Mike McLernon's story break open fresh vision for you. Mike had a master's degree in electrical engineering and was faithfully serving as a pillar of his local church in Virginia. In fact he was serving so faithfully that the pastors began to wonder if Mike had a pastoral call on his life. When a position opened up that seemed to fit his gifts, a thoughtful exploration process began that ultimately resulted in the church offering it to him. To accept the position, Mike would have to leave his profession and let go of an idea in the back of his mind that he might return one day to his native New England to plant a church. But Mike loved his church and after serious prayer and counseling, accepted the position. End of story, right? We'll let Mike tell it.

> Although I made an informed, thoughtfully considered decision to enter pastoral ministry, I quickly found that pastoring was much more difficult than I had imagined. I did not anticipate all the administrative work that was involved, and I found it hard to adjust to a pastor's schedule, with its many evening meetings and Saturday workdays. More importantly, I realized that I didn't care for people to a level that a pastor must have.
>
> After some months in my pastoral role, I began to question whether or not I really was called to full-time ministry. Eventually I summoned the courage to tell our senior pastor of my doubts about ministry. He began a lengthy process of thoughtful, caring evaluation of my gifting and character that bore much fruit. During this time I continued to be faithful in ministry, even while wondering if this was my long-term future. I recall going home many evenings thinking, "Well, I'm called to the ministry today. We'll see about tomorrow."
>
> Eventually the results of the evaluation revealed that I excelled in faithfulness in ministry, but not in the fruit that

would indicate a clear pastoral call. Everyone involved agreed that it would be better for me, my family, and the church if I left the staff and returned to the marketplace.

Rather than being disappointed at the prospect of leaving full-time ministry, I realized that my dormant dream of church planting in New England once again became possible—even though there were no plans on the horizon.

· · · · · · · · · · · · · · · · ·

See it as God's kind redirection.

· · · · · · · · · · · · · · · · ·

In the providence of God, a way opened for Mike to pursue his church-planting dream for New England in 2001. Mike joined the church-planting team as the man who could get a good job in engineering and be an anchor for the work in its formative years. Ever since then he has used his considerable gifts to do what needs to be done to build the church. He loves serving his pastors in the mission of the gospel. And Mike has learned something that every man who really wants to serve God's purpose in the church needs to know. As Mike says it,

> A man does not need a named role in a church for him to exercise genuine ministry. As he loves God's church and God's people, as he cares about their joys and sorrows, as he points them to God's compassion, then he has a real impact in the church. This occurs whether or not the man serves in an "official" capacity in the church.

Throughout this book you've read stories of great men summoned to pastoral ministry. But I think they all would look to guys like Mike and say, "That's true greatness! That's a summons story worth telling!" I know it's a story I love to tell.

A Different Door

If you're seeing the summons door closing, guess what? I've got another door you should take a look at. It's the deacon door. The deaconate is a biblically recognized office in the church. While deacons have historically served the church in a wide variety of ways, the Bible makes it clear that the church needs them.

Deacons are often found among those considering eldership. Their character and heart for the church presses the eldership question forward, but their lack of teaching gift creates an immovable obstacle. What's a guy to do? Well, think deacon! Churches are built on the shoulders of these dudes. No church will prevail without them.

Often behind the scenes, deacons fill an invaluable role in freeing pastors to do the work of preaching and teaching. While deacons are often occupied with the material needs of the church, Scripture appears to grant freedom to interpret their responsibility broadly. As one author puts it, "It seems best to view the deacons as servants who do whatever is necessary to allow the elders to accomplish their God-given calling of shepherding and teaching the church."[5] This might include taking care of the church's financial and administrative affairs, caring for the poor, leading small groups, or a wide variety of other important tasks.

You probably already have deacons in your church. They may be called something else, but whatever their title, they're the difference makers. They release the pastors, serve the people, and become the glue that helps the church stick together. And God holds out special commendation for them: "For those who serve well as deacons gain a good standing for themselves and also great confidence in the faith that is in Christ Jesus" (1 Tim. 3:13). If you're not called to be a pastor, set your ambitions on being a deacon. Your church needs you.

Perseverance and Faith

This book is the most important thing I'll ever write. That's not to say that I think it's particularly well written or destined for best-selling status—that's not my concern. But if you love the church, you have to be concerned for how it is led and how its leaders are chosen. The mission of the gospel demands nothing less than our best when it comes to helping men hear and respond to the summons.

If you're truly called, the gulf between your present situation and the full launching into your calling *will* eventually be crossed. I've tried in these pages to give you ways to extend that bridge, but only God can determine the timing of your passage. Until then . . . love God. Serve others. Study the gospel. Invest in your local church. Grow in grace. Trust God's timing. And leave the rest to God.

The ultimate test of a called man is whether he desires the advancement of the gospel more than the advancement of his own ministry. This is his constant, daily test, whether he hopes to be in ministry someday or has been in ministry for forty years. He will pass it, one last and final time, only when he passes from this earth to be with the Savior, who called him and made him faithful to that call.

We need to take to heart the words of Charles Spurgeon:

> There will be somebody to carry on the work of the Lord; and so long as the work goes on, what matter who does it? God buries the workmen, but the devil himself cannot bury the work. The work is everlasting, though the workmen die. We pass away, as star by star grows dim; but the eternal light is never fading. God shall have the victory. His Son shall come in his glory. His Spirit shall be poured out among the people; and though it be neither this man, nor that, nor the other, God will find the man to the world's end who will carry on his cause, and give him the glory.[6]

The Caller speaks. His summons rings clear. His mission is glorious. His church is his joy. May God help you hear the call and exalt the Caller.

For Additional Study
The Art of Divine Contentment, Thomas Watson
Rescuing Ambition, Dave Harvey
Trusting God, Jerry Bridges

Afterword

. . . .

For over thirty years I was part of Sovereign Grace Churches. Although I am no longer a part of this ministry, I would be remiss if I didn't acknowledge the wonderful role Sovereign Grace played in helping me develop this material, much of which was sharpened and written in my role serving Sovereign Grace Churches. And Sovereign Grace continues to be involved in church planting. If you want to know more, you can check out the church planting page on their website. I'm deeply grateful for the time I spent in Sovereign Grace, and for the many friends there who are dear to my heart.

Acknowledgments

· · · · · · · · · · · · · · · · ·

Someone once said originality is the art of concealing one's sources. Since I figure most of my thoughts are borrowed from somewhere, it seems only right to implicate the people who helped shape them into this book. So here's the line up, and I thank God for every one of them:

Andy Farmer, whose idea for the summons stories and whose editorial assistance in the entire project simply illustrate his heart to serve his friend. Thank you, A. J.

Erin Radano, the exceptional secretary who will soon depart to enjoy her promotion to motherhood. Your help on this project caps seven years of tireless service. Words can hardly capture the gratitude I feel.

Sarah, resident editor at Sovereign Grace Ministries. Thanks for loaning your eye and keyboard toward upgrading this project.

The Crossway team. I'm so grateful for your vision for this book and your desire to partner with me in publishing.

Matt Chandler somehow fit writing the foreword into his demanding life. Thank you, Matt, for serving me this way. Thanks even more for your example of suffering for God's glory.

Thomas Womack, who delivered again with his keen

theological mind and experienced editorial hand. Thanks for giving your life to improving the work of others.

Rob Flood and Jared Mellinger, who both cared enough to lend insight and talent to the effort. Thank you, my friends.

Jeff Purswell was kind enough to do a theological review. Thank you, buddy.

And lastly—but most importantly—I thank God for my bride, Kimm, who has made twenty-six years of ministry a delightful adventure together.

Notes

· · · · · · · · · · · · · · · ·

Chapter 1: The Summons As I See It

1. Charles H. Spurgeon, as quoted in James M. George, "The Call to Pastoral Ministry," in *Rediscovering Pastoral Ministry: Shaping Contemporary Ministry with Biblical Mandates,* ed. John MacArthur Jr. (Dallas, TX: Word, 1995), 103–104.

2. I use the term 'requirements' rather than the more popular use of 'qualifications' to help readers avoid seeing the lists in 1 Tim. 3 and Titus 1 as a catalog of 'disqualifying' sins. In other words, we must protect both the Church and the elders from stringent applications of these lists that may result in men immediately threatened with disqualification for nonconformance in some areas. To use 1 Tim. 3 or Titus 1 in that way is to drift from Paul's intended purpose of those passages—to offer a way to help evaluate men aspiring to ministry.

3. Some would say Luther is an exception, since he wasn't formally designated as the pastor at Wittenberg. But this was due only to his extra-local responsibilities; he remained settled in Wittenberg his entire ministry and preached at the church several times a week.

A Summons Story: Thomas Scott: Called to Conversion

1. Thomas Scott's story is adapted from Jonathan Aitken's *John Newton: From Disgrace to Amazing Grace* (Wheaton, IL: Crossway, 2007) and from *Letters of John Newton* (Carlisle, PA: Banner of Truth, 2007).

Chapter 2: Summoned to the Savior

1. I'm indebted for the concept of the Caller to Os Guinness, who makes a passing reference to God as "Caller" in his book, *The Call: Finding and Fulfilling the Central Purpose of Your Life* (Nashville, TN: Word, 1998), 93.

2. Sinclair Ferguson, *The Christian Life: A Doctrinal Introduction* (Edinburgh, Scotland: Banner of Truth, 1997), 33.

3. Wayne Grudem, *Bible Doctrine: Essential Teachings of the Christian Faith* (Grand Rapids, MI: Zondervan, 1999), 296.

4. Charles H. Spurgeon, as quoted in John Piper, *The Pleasures of God: Meditations on God's Delight in Being God* (Portland, OR: Multnomah, 1991), 125–26.

5. Edmund P. Clowney, *Called to the Ministry* (Phillipsburg, NJ: P&R, 1964), 5.

6. Guinness, *The Call*, 31.

7. "What's an old vase worth?" *The Week*, November 18, 2010. Accessed April 22, 2011. http://theweek.com/article/index/209511/a-homeless-man-charms-oprah-and-more.

A Summons Story: Charles Simeon: Called to the Church

1. Charles Simeon's story is adapted from Handley C. G. Moule's *Charles Simeon, Pastor of a Generation* (London: Methuen, 1892); and from John Piper, "Brothers, We Must Not Mind a Little Suffering" (message, at the 1989 Bethlehem Conference for Pastors). Accessed April 2, 2011, at http://www.desiringgod.org/resource-library/biographies/brothers-we-must-not-mind-a-little-suffering.

2. Quoted by Moule in *Charles Simeon*, 36.

Chapter 3: The Context of the Call

1. Robert L. Withers, "Pastoral Transitions and Longevity," Compass Dynamics, accessed April 5, 2011, http://www.compassdynamics.org/pastoral-transitions.html.

2. Brian Croft, *Test, Train, Affirm, and Send into Ministry: Recovering the Local Church's Responsibility in the External Call* (Leominster, UK: Day One, 2010), 47–48.

3. Richard Baxter, *The Reformed Pastor* (Portland, OR: Multnomah, 1982), 69.

4. John Piper, *Brothers, We Are Not Professionals: A Plea to Pastors for Radical Ministry* (Nashville, TN: Broadman, 2002), 3.

5. David Wells, "The D-Min-Ization of the Ministry," in *No God but God: Breaking with the Idols of Our Age*, ed. Os Guinness and John Seel (Chicago, IL: Moody, 1992), 175 (footnote).

6. Edmund Venables, *The Life of John Bunyan* (London: Walter Scott, 1888), 117.

7. Dr. Albert Mohler of Southern Baptist Theological Seminary in Louisville, Kentucky. The following quote is from an online interview by Adrian Warnock, as accessed April 6, 2011, at http://adrianwarnock.com/2008/01/22nd-most-read-post-dr-albert-mohler/.

A Summons Story: Lemuel Haynes: Called to Godliness

1. Lemuel Haynes's story is adapted from Thabiti Anyabwile, *The Faithful Preacher: Recapturing the Vision of Three Pioneering African-American Pastors* (Wheaton, IL: Crossway, 2007), and from the Online PBS series "Africans in America" at http://www.pbs.org/wgbh/aia/part2/2p29.html, accessed April 6, 2011.

2. Anyabwile, *The Faithful Preacher*, 21.

3. Lemuel Haynes, from the sermon, "The Character and Work of a Spiritual Watchman Described" (1792), as presented in Anyabwile, *The Faithful Preacher*, 34–35.

Chapter 4: Are You Godly?

1. Aubrey Malphurs sees no reason to separate the requirements for an elder from that of a church planter. He writes, "These are the requirements for elders but are also essential for church planters." In *Planting Growing Churches for the 21st Century: A Comprehensive Guide for New Churches and Those Desiring Renewal* (Grand Rapids, MI: Baker, 2004), 111.

2. As already stated it's wiser, not to mention nearer to the original intent of 1 Timothy 3 and Titus 1, to use the word "requirements" rather than "qualifications." Since the first use of these passages is to evaluate men not yet in ministry, employing the term "qualifications" opens the door to misapplication for men already in ministry, and implies that an ordained pastor with a weakness in any given area may be immediately deserving of disqualification.

3. Joel Nederhood, "The Minister's Call," in *The Preacher and Preaching,* Samuel T. Logan, ed. (Phillipsburg, NJ: P&R, 1986), 39.

4. "Very importantly, the controlling verbs of all the requirements of the overseer listed in 1 Tim 3:2-6 are all Present tense. They are *dei* <Pres Act Ind 3 Sg> = 'it is necessary,' and . . . *einai* <Pres Act Infin> = 'to be' in 3:2." George W. Knight, *The Pastoral Epistles: A Commentary on the Greek Text*, New International Greek Testament Commentary (Grand Rapids, MI: Eerdmans, 1992), 160.

5. From the sermon "Zeal an Essential Virtue of a Christian," in *Sermons and Discourses, 1739–1742*, vol. 22 in *The Works of Jonathan Edwards* (New Haven, CT: Yale University Press, 2003), 144; as quoted by Dane Ortlund in *A New Inner Relish: Christian Motivation in the Thought of Jonathan Edwards* (Tain, Scotland: Christian Focus, 2008), 120.

6. Jeff Purswell, "How Do I Know If I'm Called? (lecture, New Attitude Conference, 2002). Message can be accessed on *New Attitude Five 45* audio CD. http://www.sovereigngracestore.com/ProductInfo.aspx?productid=A2120-00-22.

7. John Piper, *Finally Alive* (Tain, Scotland: Christian Focus, 2009), 191.

8. Alexander Strauch, *Biblical Eldership* (Littleton, CO: Lewis & Roth, 1995), 188.

9. James M. George, "The Call to Pastoral Ministry," in *Rediscovering Pastoral Ministry: Shaping Pastoral Ministry with Biblical Mandates*, ed. John MacArthur Jr. (Nashville, TN: Thomas Nelson, 1995), 114.

10. Charles R. Swindoll, *The Bride: Renewing Our Passion for the Church* (Grand Rapids, MI: Zondervan, 1994), 171.

11. D. A. Carson, *A Call to Spiritual Reformation: Priorities from Paul and His Prayers* (Grand Rapids, MI: Baker, 1992), 83.

12. John MacArthur Jr., quoted in Alexander Strauch, *Biblical Eldership*, 70.

A Summons Story: Martin Luther: Modeling the Pastoral Home

1. Luther's story is adapted from Roland Bainton's *Here I Stand: A Life of Martin Luther* (NY: Abington, 1977), 223–37 and from William J. Petersen, *25 Surprising Marriages: Faith-Building Stories from the Lives of Famous Christians* (Grand Rapids, MI: 1997), 151–165.

2. Petersen, 25 *Surprising Marriages*, 164.

3. Martin Luther, *Table Talk* (1539).

4. Paul Thigpen, "A Family Album," *Christian History*, July 1, 1993.

5. As quoted by Roland Bainton in *Here I Stand*, 236.

6. Martin Luther, as quoted by Steven Ozment, "Reinventing Family Life," in *Christian History*, July 1, 1993.

Chapter 5: How's Your Home?

1. It's essential to realize that the primary purpose of 1 Timothy 3:1-7 and Titus 1:6-9 is to identify potential elders, not for evaluating or disqualifying existing elders. This does not imply they have no relevance, but simply acknowledges the original intent of the text. For understanding the discipline and disqualification of elders, a more important passage and practice is found in 1 Timothy 5:19-21, which exists to both protect elders from frivolous charges while also ensuring a congregation has recourse against elders engaged in misconduct.

2. John Kitchen, *The Pastoral Epistles for Pastors* (Woodlands, TX: Kress, 2009), 132.

3. John MacArthur Jr., "The Character of a Pastor," in *Rediscovering Pastoral Ministry: Shaping Pastoral Ministry with Biblical Mandates*, ed. John MacArthur Jr. (Nashville, TN: Thomas Nelson, 1995), 91.

4. *ESV Study Bible* (Wheaton, IL: Crossway, 2008), at 1 Timothy 3:4–5.

5. "Negatively, the phrase prohibits all deviation from faithful, monogamous marriage." Alexander Strauch, *Biblical Eldership* (Littleton, CO: Lewis & Roth), 192. For additional study on this point, see John Calvin's perspective on these passages in his commentaries on the Pastoral Epistles (available in various editions); George W. Knight, *The Pastoral Epistles*, New International Greek Testament Commentary (Grand Rapids, MI: Eerdmans, 1992), 157–58; and William Mounce, *Pastoral Epistles*, vol. 46 in Word Biblical Commentary, ed. Bruce M. Metzger (Nashville, TN: Thomas Nelson, 2000), 170–73.

6. Gordon D. Fee, *1 and 2 Timothy, Titus*, vol. 13 in the New International Biblical Commentary, ed. W. Ward Gasque (Peabody, MA: Hendrickson), 80.

7. Charles Bridges, *The Christian Ministry* (London: Seeley and Burnside, 1830), 169.

8. George W. Knight, in his commentary on Titus 1:6 in *The Pastoral Epistles*, suggests that the qualifying description of children here "means 'faithful' in the sense of 'submissive' or 'obedient,' as a servant or steward is regarded… when he carries out the requests of his master." Knight acknowledges that "this proposed understanding goes contrary to a consistent pattern in recent English translation . . . but the considerations above seem compelling," 290.

9. "The contrast is made not between believing and unbelieving children, but between obedient, respectful children and lawless, uncontrolled children." Strauch, *Biblical Eldership*, 229. What is at stake, Strauch suggests, is "the children's behavior, not their eternal state."

10. D. A. Carson: "As long as the children are under their father's roof, the bishop/elder must so order his household as to demonstrate he is capable

of ordering the church." Carson, *For the Love of God* (Wheaton, IL: Crossway, 1998), reading for November 2. John R. W. Stott: "The text suggests that Paul has childhood in mind. For, although *tekna* ('children') could be used of posterity in general and occasionally of grown adults, it usually refers to youngsters who are still in their minority (which of course varies in different cultures) and are therefore regarded as being still under their parents' authority." Stott, *Guard the Truth: The Message of 1 Timothy and Titus* (Carol Stream, IL: InterVarsity, 1996), 176.

11. John Piper, "Should a Pastor Continue in Ministry if One of His Children Proves to Be an Unbeliever?" (sermon, Bethlehem Baptist Church, May 15, 2009). Accessed January 28, 2011, at http://www.desiringgod.org/resource-library/ask-pastor-john/should-a-pastor-continue-in-ministry-if-one-of-his-children-proves-to-be-an-unbeliever.

12. Bridges, *The Christian Ministry*, 166.

13. Vern Sheridan Poythress, "The Church as Family: Why Male Leadership in the Family Requires Male Leadership in the Church," in *Recovering Biblical Manhood and Womanhood*, eds. Wayne Grudem and John Piper (Wheaton, IL: Crossway, 2006), 235.

A Summons Story: David Martyn Lloyd-Jones: Called to Preach

1. Lloyd-Jones's story is adapted from Iain Murray's *D. Martyn Lloyd-Jones: The First Forty Years* (Edinburgh: Banner of Truth, 1982).

2. As quoted by Murray, *D. Martyn Lloyd-Jones*, 80.

Chapter 6: Can You Preach?

1. Charles H. Spurgeon, as quoted by Fred Smith in *Learning to Lead: How to Bring Out the Best in People* (Waco, TX: Word, 1986), 23.

2. Matt. 4:17; Mark 1:14; Luke 4:43; Acts 14:21–22; 1 Cor. 1:17–25; 1 Tim. 4:13–14; and 2 Tim. 4:1–4, to name just a few passages.

3. John MacArthur Jr., "Preaching" in *Rediscovering Pastoral Ministry: Shaping Pastoral Ministry with Biblical Mandates*, ed. John MacArthur Jr. (Dallas, TX: Word, 1995), 250.

4. Charles H. Spurgeon, *Lectures to My Students* (London: Passmore and Alabaster, 1877), 28.

5. D. A. Carson, quoting a Mennonite leader, in Melvin Tinker's *Reversal or Betrayal?* (Lewes, UK: Berith, 1999), 271.

6. John Calvin, commentary on John 3:29, as quoted by Charles Bridges, *The Christian Ministry* (London: Seeley and Burnside, 1830), 15.

7. Quoted in Darrell W. Johnson, *The Glory of Preaching: Participating in God's Transformation of the World* (Downers Grove, IL: InterVarsity, 2009), 172.

8. *Oratio, meditatio, tentatio faciunt theologum*—this was a frequent theme with Luther. For example, in the preface to the Wittenberg Edition of Luther's writings (1539), he states that in Psalm 119 we "find three rules, amply presented throughout the whole Psalm. They are *Oratio, Meditatio, Tentatio*."

9. John Piper, "Brothers, Our Affliction Is for Their Comfort," in *The Standard*, December 1982, 28–29.

10. Charles L. Chaney, *Church Planting at the End of the Twentieth Century* (Carol Stream, IL: Tyndale, 1993), 227.

A Summons Story: James Montgomery Boice: A Shepherd in the City

1. Boice's story was composed using information from the Tenth Presbyterian Church website, http://www.tenth.org, the ACE website, http://www.alliancenet.org, and the website at monergism.com, http://www.monergism.com/thethreshold/articles/bio/jamesmboice.html.

2. "A Long History," *This People, This Place*, Tenth Presbyterian Church, accessed December 13, 2011, http://www.tenth.org/index.php?id=334&no_cache=1&tx_bddbflvvideogallery_pi[video]=1.

3. "Dr. Boice's Testimony," Tenth Presbyterian Church, accessed December 13, 2011, http://www.tenth.org/index.php?id=364.

Chapter 7: Can You Shepherd?

1. Timothy Z. Witmer, *The Shepherd Leader: Achieving Effective Shepherding in Your Church* (Phillipsburg, NJ: P&R, 2010), 2.

2. Timothy Laniak, *Shepherds After My Own Heart: Pastoral Traditions and Leadership in the Bible* (Downers Grove, IL: InterVarsity, 2006), 233.

3. D. Martyn Lloyd-Jones, *Preaching and Preachers* (Grand Rapids, MI: Zondervan, 1971), 92, quoted in Irvin A. Busenitz, "Training for Pastoral Ministry," in *Rediscovering Pastoral Ministry: Shaping Pastoral Ministry with Biblical Mandates*, ed. John MacArthur Jr. (Nashville, TN: Thomas Nelson, 1995), 131–32.

4. "One of the primary metaphors by which biblical authors conceptualized leadership is shepherding." Laniak, *Shepherds After My Own Heart* (Downers Grove, IL: InterVarsity, 2006), 21.

5. Ralph C. Wood, in "Why Pastors Leave Parish Ministry," a book review for The Christian Century Foundation of the book *Pastors in Transition: Why Clergy Leave Local Church Ministry* by Dean B. Hoge and Jacqueline E. Wenger. Wood cites statistics reported by Hoge and Wenger. His review accessed April 7, 2011, at http://www.religion-online.org/showarticle.asp?title=3319.

6. Wood, "Why Pastors Leave Parish Ministry."

7. Alexander Strauch, *Biblical Eldership* (Littleton, CO: Lewis & Roth, 1995), 37.

8. Except when referring to a specific elder (1 Tim. 5:19; 1 Pet. 5:1), the New Testament's usage is always plural.

9. J. L. Reynolds, "Church Polity or the Kingdom of Christ," in *Polity: Biblical Arguments on How to Conduct Church Life (A Collection of Historic Baptist Documents)*, Mark E. Dever, ed. (Washington, DC: Center for Church Reform; Nine Marks Ministries, 2001), 349.

10. Strauch, *Biblical Eldership*, 37.

11. Wayne Grudem said, "The pastor of the church will be one of the elders in the session (the body of elders in a Reformed church), *equal in authority to the other elders*. This session has *governing authority* over the local church" (empha-

sis mine). Wayne Grudem, *Systematic Theology: An Introduction to Biblical Doctrine* (Grand Rapids, MI: Zondervan, 1994), 925–26.

12. Edmund Clowney, *The Message of 1 Peter*, (Downers Grove, IL: InterVarsity, 1988), 198.

13. Paul Johnson, (lecture, Covenant Fellowship Church, Glen Mills, PA, October 16, 2004).

A Summons Story: Charles Spurgeon: Loving the Lost

1. Spurgeon's story is adapted from Lewis Drummond's *Spurgeon: Prince of Preachers* (Grand Rapids, MI: Kregel, 1992), and from Tom Ascol's "A Lesson from Spurgeon on Evangelism" in *Founders Journal* (published by Founders Ministries SBC), Issue 33 (http://www.founders.org/journal/fj33/editorial.html; accessed April 7, 2011).

2. Stephen Nichols, as quoted by Drummond in *Spurgeon: Prince of Preachers*, 29.

3. As quoted by Tom Ascol, "A Lesson from Spurgeon on Evangelism."

4. As quoted by Drummond, *Spurgeon: Prince of Preachers*, 29.

5. As quoted by Tom Ascol, "A Lesson from Spurgeon on Evangelism."

Chapter 8: Do You Love the Lost?

1. Mark Dever, *Dear Timothy* (Cape Coral, FL: Founders, 2004), 158–59.

2. I'm grateful for a message I heard on this passage by Ed Stetzer. While the chapter content is not drawn from Ed's message, the organization of it is.

3. Michael P. Green, ed., *Illustrations for Biblical Preaching* (Grand Rapids, MI: Baker, 1989), 62.

4. Wayne Grudem, *Systematic Theology: An Introduction to Biblical Doctrine* (Grand Rapids, MI: Zondervan, 2000), 868.

5. William Chadwick, *Stealing Sheep: The Church's Hidden Problem with Transfer Growth* (Downers Grove, IL: InterVarsity, 2001), 10.

6. Note this observation by Aubrey Malphurs in *Planting Growing Churches for the 21st Century: A Comprehensive Guide for New Churches and Those Desiring Renewal* (Grand Rapids, MI: Baker, 1998), 64.

7. Colin Marshall and Tony Payne, *The Trellis and the Vine: The Ministry Mind-Shift that Changes Everything* (Kingsford, Australia: Matthias Media, 2009), 107.

8. Joseph Thayer, "2229 εὐαγγελιστής," *Thayer's Greek-English Lexicon of the New Testament* (June 1996), quoted in Bibleworks, 8th ed. CD-ROM, version 1.0 (Bibleworks LLC, 2004).

9. Charles H. Spurgeon, *Lectures to My Students* (London: Passmore and Alabaster, 1877), 180.

A Summons Story: John Bunyan: A Calling Confirmed by the Church

1. Bunyan's story is adapted from his *Grace Abounding to the Chief of Sinners* (Collected Works, Vol. 8, Ages Digital Library), and from Frank Mott Harrison, *John Bunyan* (Edinburgh: Banner of Truth, 1964).

2. Bunyan, *Grace Abounding to the Chief of Sinners*.

3. Ibid.

Chapter 9: Who Agrees?

1. Charles H. Spurgeon, *Lectures to My Students* (London: Passmore and Alabaster, 1877), 25.

2. Charles Bridges, *The Christian Ministry* (London: Seeley and Burnside, 1830), 91–92.

3. Ibid.

4. Consider that 1 Timothy is written first to Timothy in his leadership role. Titus, in similar fashion, was being asked to identify and appoint elders. The future of the church rests upon leaders selecting, training, and confirming future elders (1 Tim. 5:22; 2 Tim. 2:2).

5. Bridges, *The Christian Ministry*, 90 (emphasis mine).

6. The nineteenth-century Baptist theologian J. L. Dagg asserted that any man who was alone in believing God called him to ministry "has reason to apprehend that he is under delusion." Dagg added that if those who "honor God and love the souls of men" aren't recognizing a man's ministry requirements, that man "has reason to suspect that they do not exist." As quoted by Brian Croft in *Test, Train, Affirm, and Send into Ministry: Recovering the Local Church's Responsibility in the External Call* (Leominster, UK: Day One, 2010), 51.

7. G. Campbell Morgan, *The Acts of the Apostles*, ed. D. Stuart Briscoe (Grand Rapids, MI: Revell, 1988), 242.

8. Charles H. Spurgeon, as quoted by John MacArthur Jr. in *Rediscovering Pastoral Ministry: Shaping Pastoral Ministry with Biblical Mandates* (Nashville, TN: Thomas Nelson, 1995), 103–104.

9. Oswald Sanders, as quoted in Henry Blackaby and Richard Blackaby, *Spiritual Leadership: Moving People on to God's Agenda* (Nashville, TN: Broadman, 2001), 88.

10. Charles H. Spurgeon, as quoted by Lewis Drummond's *Spurgeon: Prince of Preachers* (Grand Rapids, MI: Kregel, 1992), 200.

A Summons Story: John Newton: Knowing the Value of Waiting

1. Newton's story is adapted from Jonathan Aitken's *John Newton: From Disgrace to Amazing Grace* (Wheaton, IL: Crossway, 2007) and from *Letters of John Newton* (Edinburgh: Banner of Truth, 2007).

2. Quoted by Aitken in *John Newton*, 159.

3. From a letter dated March 7, 1765. John Newton, *Voice of the Heart*, ed. Jay P. Green Sr. (Lafayette, IN: Sovereign Grace, Inc., 2001), 137–38.

Chapter 10: While You Wait

1. George Herbert, as quoted by Charles Bridges, *The Christian Ministry* (London: Seeley and Burnside, 1830), 62.

2. Wayne Grudem, *Systematic Theology: An Introduction to Biblical Doctrine* (Grand Rapids, MI: Zondervan, 1994), 916.

3. Charles H. Spurgeon, *Exploring the Mind & Heart of the Prince of Preachers* (Oswego, IL: Fox River, 2005), M–503.

4. Quoted by James M. Garretson in *Princeton and Preaching* (Carlisle, PA: Banner of Truth, 2005), 45.

5. Benjamin L. Merkle, *40 Questions About Elders and Deacons* (Grand Rapids, MI: Kregel, 2008), 240.

6. Charles H. Spurgeon, *Metropolitan Tabernacle Pulpit*, 1892, vol. 38, p. 297.